The Way of Presence

ENDORSEMENTS

"*The Way of Presence* is a wonderfully insightful invitation to go beyond merely seeking truth intellectually in exchange for a daily practice of pursuing lived wisdom in grace. Alan Fadling has a way of writing that gives room for the reader who seeks to open their heart so that they may abide in the reality of God's presence. Fadling's wisdom has been a great encouragement to me ever since I stumbled upon *An Unhurried Life* at my local library, and I know this book will speak to many others in the same way."

MORGAN HARPER NICHOLS
Artist and poet; author of All Along You Were Blooming

"Once again Alan writes with remarkable clarity and evident wisdom, reminding us that Jesus as the way, the truth, and the life is not simply a glib recitation of a Bible verse. Instead it is an accessible invitation to a life of vitality, intimacy, and flourishing. Free from rote answers, lazy Christian clichés, and limp questions, his wise insight and incisive questions are valuable tools for the adventure with Jesus. Alan provides mini personal retreats that point us in the best direction of all: toward the heart of the Father."

J. R. Briggs
Founder, Kairos Partnerships; author, The Sacred Overlap: Learning to Live Faithfully in the Space Between

"Alan Fadling's *Way of Presence* is like a gift box full of spiritual nuggets, with thoughts and questions that will leave you pondering for the rest of the day. If you want something to stimulate growth in your soul, open it up and settle down with this collection of real-life lessons straight from the heart."

Andrea Buczynski
VP of Global Leadership Development, Cru

"Alan Fadling once again brings thoughtfulness, attentiveness to the Spirit, and a gracious practicality to his reflections on life and Scripture. This is a helpful resource for anyone looking for a daily reflection guide that both soothes the soul and challenges the spirit to press further into the journey of spiritual formation. Well worth your time and energy."

Casey Tygrett
Pastor, spiritual director, and author of As I Recall: Discovering the Place of Memories in Our Spiritual Life

"One thing I appreciate about Alan Fadling's approach to unhurried living and to these daily readings is not that we find rest through escape but that we experience rest when we sink more deeply into reality. When we remind ourselves that reality is found in God's presence, we can begin to unhurry. These brief readings and reflective questions offer us gentle guidance into the way, the truth and the life."

CINDY BUNCH
Author of Be Kind to Yourself

"Alan Fadling has quite a few groupies in the world who follow everything he writes. I'm one of them. Fadling's new book *The Way of Presence* is an absolute joy to endorse as I know it's impact on me will be the same as everything else he's written—deep and transformative. Fadling finds the most creative ways to help us slow down and simply enjoy God. This book will move your soul. Read it—slowly."

A. J. SWOBODA, PHD
Assistant Professor of Bible, Theology, and World Christianity at Bushnell University; author, Subversive Sabbath

OTHER BOOKS BY ALAN FADLING

An Unhurried Life

An Unhurried Leader

Inhaling Grace

What Does Your Soul Love? (with Gem Fadling)

The Way of Presence

THE EMPOWERING REALITY OF GOD-WITH-US

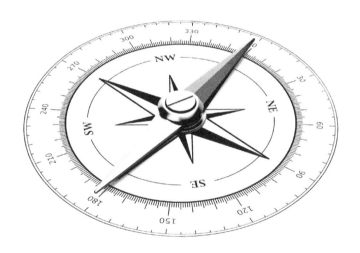

by Alan Fadling

Published by Unhurried Living

While any stories in this book are true, some names and identifying information may have been changed to protect the privacy of individuals.

Cover & interior design: Kirsten Doukas, Pastel Black Design.

Print ISBN: 978-1-7352668-2-4
Ebook ISBN: 978-1-7352668-3-1

Printed in the United States of America

CONTENTS

CONTENTS

CONTENTS

ACKNOWLEDGMENTS

On the morning I finished the first draft of this book, we were coming to the end of our first week of being asked to stay home because of concerns about COVID-19 and its spread. It happened to be the fourth Sunday of Lent.

A number of my speaking engagements had already been cancelled, and the financial impact was proving to be fairly significant. On that morning, Unhurried Living saw a large donation from an unexpected source who shared she had awakened in the night with a thought. She remembered an old account with money in it and felt a nudge to give it to Unhurried Living. She wanted us to know God loves us and sees us, and she believes in the work we are doing. She shared her conviction that what we do is even more needed in these difficult times.

To this donor I say "Thank you," and I acknowledge the ways in which God used you to make this project and my work in that season possible.

INTRODUCTION

At some point early in my new life as a Christian, I remember hearing the well-known words of Jesus as he spoke with his inner circle in the upper room on that last night they would share together before his arrest, trial, suffering, and crucifixion. Recorded in John 14:6, Jesus says, "I am the way, the truth, and the life." In my early Christian life those words were taught as something I needed to agree with and tell other people about. That's not a bad place to start, but I've been grateful to grow in discovering the depths of what Jesus says about himself here. Jesus as way, truth, and life are avenues of engagement with him, a vital journey for the whole of our lives.

One of my favorite Eugene Peterson lines comes at the beginning of his book *The Jesus Way:*

> *I am the way, the truth, and the life" (John 14:6). The Jesus way wedded to the Jesus truth brings about the Jesus life. We can't proclaim the Jesus truth but then do it any old way we like. Nor can we follow the Jesus way without speaking the Jesus truth. . . . We can't suppress the Jesus way in order to sell the Jesus truth. The Jesus way and the Jesus truth must*

be congruent. Only when the Jesus way is organically joined with the Jesus truth do we get the Jesus life.*

This integration of the truth of Jesus lived in the way of Jesus leading to the life of Jesus in us and among us has been such a gift to me. The truth of Jesus isn't simply something to be affirmed as a statement of faith external to me.

Jesus as truth speaks of Jesus as our guide to that which is real. Jesus is our reference point, our north star, our guiding mentor. What Jesus says is wise guidance for our lived reality. Truth is more than right answers. It is lived wisdom. Jesus *is* the truth. The "I am" of Jesus is our reality—the kingdom in which we live.

Jesus as life speaks to finding our vitality, our energy, and our joy in him. Rather than saying "*this* is the life," as though there were something out there somewhere that brings me life, I say, "*Jesus* is my life." Maybe that sounds a little too religious to some people's ears, but this has been a growing reality in my life. Christ *is* my life.

But of the three descriptors in John 14:6, I think Jesus as way gets the least attention. We often focus on the teachings of Je-

---

* Eugene Peterson, The Jesus Way (Grand Rapids: Eerdmans, 2007), 4, 6–7.

sus ("the truth") and the gift of eternal life in Jesus ("the life"), but not as much on how Jesus does what he does or *how* Jesus actually lives his life ("the way"). Jesus as way speaks to me of a journey we take, a path on which we walk, a companionship that we cultivate, and an ongoing interactive experience. Day by day, moment by moment, we are on the way with Christ.

In all three of these, I encounter Jesus as "I am." Jesus being the way, the truth, and the life is more than just a theological fact about him. It is a vital and organic reality. I walk with Jesus as the way. I see myself through the eyes of Jesus as the truth. I live my every moment in communion with Jesus as the life. The whole Christian life is an experience with Jesus as way, truth, and life.

When I first wrote *Inhaling Grace,* I gave it the subtitle "A 60-Day Unhurried Living Devotional." With the release of *The Way of Presence,* which I intend as its sequel, I've moved away from that "devotional" label. I realize that I rarely read devotionals, and of the ones I've read most recently, some felt a bit like predigested inspiration that didn't ask much of me. That's not what I've sought to do in these pages.

Of course, not all devotionals are like that. There have been seasons in my life when *My Utmost for His Highest* by Oswald Chambers was like a daily spiritual guide, showing me the way forward in my journey with God. I felt I had a wise companion walking alongside me each day. Each reading felt like just enough light to take my next step well.

I've imagined these sixty brief chapters as five-minute retreats, not in the sense of escaping reality but of sinking more deeply *into* reality. I crafted the questions at the end of each chapter to help you take a moment to sink into the real presence of God as you read. My hope is that these readings would somehow, like Jesus himself, be full of both grace and truth. Grace without truth is simply unchallenging inspiration. Truth without grace is unbending advice that we're left to figure out on our own. Grace and truth overflowing together enables us to see the path before us and find strength to walk that path in God's presence.

These sixty daily readings began as excerpts from my personal journal. As such, they represent snapshots from a season in my own life when I was seeking to make my way in the reality of Christ with me. One of the core callings that my wife, Gem, and I have sensed God extending has been to share our lives with others. Not just truths, insights, or ideas, but *life*. I pray that as you read, you'll sense the invitation of Jesus in your own life to join him in his way and abide with him in the reality of his presence.

PART 1: THE WAY OF GOD

1. GOD MEETS ME WHERE I AM

I waited patiently upon the LORD; he stooped to me and heard my cry. — Psalm 40:1

I love the imagery of the Lord stooping to me. I remember when our three sons were little. I was tall and they were short. That's how it goes with fathers and little boys. Sometimes they would come to me crying about something that had hurt or scared or frustrated them. When they came, I would sometimes stoop or even kneel down to get on eye level with them to love and comfort them. I love that David uses an image like this to describe God's response to him when he cries out.

I am down here. He is "up there." I am a little child and God is a good Father. He meets me where I am. The way of God is fatherly and gracious. Sometimes I imagine that I need to reach up to him and get his attention, as if I must jump to somehow reach him. But God reaches down to me. He leans down to meet me where I am. He hears my cries.

Unlike the image of a little boy and a father, David says that he has learned to wait patiently for the Lord to come down to him. Little ones aren't usually good at patient waiting. So David has learned to wait with some maturity and patience. This is an invitation to me. I can learn that when something in my life pressures me or stresses me, I can cry out and patiently wait for God to come to me.

God comes down to my level. I simply have to learn to be patient in my watching and waiting for him. He *will* come. He will.

- *What have you found yourself watching and waiting for lately? Has it been patient or impatient waiting?*

- *When have you been in a hard season, crying out to God? How have you experienced God stooping down to meet you there? How would you like him to meet you in it?*

2. SINNERS LOVE HIM

Now when the Pharisee who had invited him saw
it, he said to himself, "If this man were a prophet, he
would have known who and what kind of woman
this is who is touching him—that she is a sinner."
— *Luke 7:39 NRSV*

Jesus and some friends have accepted a Pharisee's invitation to dine with him in his house. What does the Pharisee see that raises such a judgmental reaction in him? As they are at the table eating, a woman of bad reputation enters the house and comes to Jesus, weeping, then actually washes his feet with her tears and dries them with her hair (Luke 7:38). She kisses his feet and anoints them with some ointment she has brought with her.

What humility and love! But that isn't what the Pharisee sees. He doesn't see this woman's heart. He can only notice how notorious her life is. Whatever she was known for—perhaps adultery or prostitution—must have made her a public outcast. The Pharisee assumes that Jesus is unaware of her status.

He also assumes that this woman will somehow pollute Jesus and that he ought to know better than to let her touch him.

The Pharisee believes in the classic "outside-in" approach to morality—something the Pharisees were famous for. But Jesus comes as a physician for those who need healing. Physicians have to be up close and personal with all kinds of illness and brokenness to be able to help. And so instead of being polluted by the woman, Jesus brings healing and forgiveness to her. She doesn't pollute him. He saves her.

- *Do you ever fear that something dirty "out there" will make you unclean?*

- *Is it possible that you actually bring the holiness and goodness of Christ with you wherever you go, and that you just might help heal the world rather than being polluted by it? Talk to God about these things for a bit.*

3. NEVER TOO LATE FOR RESURRECTION

When Mary reached the place where Jesus was and
saw him, she fell at his feet and said, "Lord, if you
had been here, my brother would not have died.
— John 11:32

My heart feels heavy when I read Mary's words, "Lord, if you had been here, my brother would not have died." I try to imagine the sadness and disappointment in her heart. She's tempted to imagine that Jesus could have shown a bit more care by arriving in time to help.

Mary is not wrong. Jesus certainly *could have* prevented Lazarus's death. He had that power. But it seems there was a deeper truth Jesus wanted Mary to experience. There was something about Jesus she didn't know. He wanted her to learn that not only could he prevent death but he could also conquer death. He wanted her to encounter him as the Resurrection and the Life. Resurrection is a greater miracle than death prevention.

When we feel disappointed by what appears to be God's failure to show up, is it possible that his intent might be to do something far greater for us than we could imagine? Might we learn something in the thirteenth hour, *after* God has seemingly failed to act on our behalf, that is greater than what we would learn if God arrived just in time to save us? The reality of resurrection requires the reality of death first.

- *Are there places in your life where you feel like God has failed to arrive in time? How do those places make you feel about God?*

- *Have you ever experienced what seemed to you like God arriving too late, only to discover that there was something more God wished to do? If so, what was that like? If not, how might you keep your eyes open to this possibility?*

4. WHEN JESUS DELAYS

When he heard this, Jesus said, "This sickness will
not end in death. No, it is for God's glory so that
God's Son may be glorified through it." — John 11:4

A messenger from Mary and Martha had reached Jesus and
told him that Lazarus, their brother and his good friend, was
sick. Jesus delays his journey to be with them and declares
that Lazarus's sickness will not end in death. And from our
vantage point, we know that Lazarus's illness did not lead to
permanent death but was rather an opportunity for Jesus to
display God's glorious healing power. But for Mary and Martha, it looks exactly like Lazarus's illness has ended in death.

Four days after Lazarus died, Jesus' words would have sounded cruel to Mary and Martha, maybe even tempting them to
think that Jesus was mistaken, or worse—that he doesn't care.
Do I ever judge Jesus in light of what looks like his lack of care
rather than trusting in his care in spite of hard circumstances?
I do sometimes.

As Jesus prepares to begin his journey to go visit Lazarus and his sisters at Bethany, he says to his disciples:

> *"Our friend Lazarus has fallen asleep; but I am going there to wake him up." His disciples replied, "Lord, if he sleeps, he will get better." Jesus had been speaking of his death, but his disciples thought he meant natural sleep. (John 11:11–13)*

Jesus speaks of Lazarus's condition with calm and peace. Though Jesus knows Lazarus's death is not permanent, this is still a remarkable thing. When Jesus speaks of sleep, the disciples understandably assume that Lazarus will wake up. But Jesus is speaking of a sleep from which no one naturally awakens. We don't hear a yawn and "Good morning!" from inside a casket at a funeral. It doesn't happen. But it *does* happen to Lazarus.

We don't usually see death in the same peaceful, trusting light as Jesus does. We don't usually see hard things with the same calm as Jesus does. But Jesus is a master teacher and is willing to mentor us in just such a perspective. That's good news in the midst of our hard situations.

- *Are you faced with any unexpected hardship or loss that you're tempted to see as evidence of God's uncaring delay?*

- *Can you imagine a future in which God's faithfulness, care, and power will surprise you with a different perspective from the one you have now?*

5. THE LORD IS NOT SLOW

But do not forget this one thing, dear friends: With the Lord a day is like a thousand years, and a thousand years are like a day. The Lord is not slow in keeping his promise, as some understand slowness. Instead he is patient with you, not wanting anyone to perish, but everyone to come to repentance.

— 2 Peter 3:8–9

"The Lord is not slow." This is an intriguing statement in comparison to the concept of unhurried living. God is not guilty of an unholy, unloving slowness. The Lord is not slow as it relates to faithfulness. What may seem slow to us is actually God's patience. His patience may look slow, but it is slow with a purpose.

A thousand years is like a day, and day is like a thousand years with God. The year 1020, when the church was only decades away from the Great Schism between East and West, is like yesterday to God. This is the direction in which I usually understand these words about God and time.

But a day is also like a thousand years. With God, a single day is so full of life that it could take us a thousand years to unpack it. A single day is dense with meaning in God. There is more kingdom life available to us in one day than we can imagine.

God isn't lackadaisical about his promises. We often assume that the delays we perceive are always bad news. But here Peter says that the delay of God is about opportunity. What we see as uncaring lateness is actually loving patience. God is always working to help us turn more fully toward him, to be more deeply rooted in him, to find our life in him. All of these things take more time than we realize.

- *Where have you been tempted to believe the Lord is slow in his faithfulness to you? What challenge in your life feels like it's been taking God too long to address or resolve?*

- *Can you envision a way in which this delay might actually be an expression of God's patient love for you and faithfulness to you? Talk with God about this.*

6. GRACE AND RIGHTEOUSNESS: NOT OIL AND WATER

The LORD is gracious and righteous; our God is
full of compassion. The LORD protects the unwary;
when I was brought low, he saved me.
—Psalm 116:5–6

What happens in my heart when I read these lines? I realize that there are young emotions within me that cannot conceive of a God who is both gracious *and* righteous. Inside is still a young child terrified of the harsh and angry God that was preached at him in the fundamentalist Christian church I attended in my childhood. (I'm pretty sure this was the sort of church my parents attended in their childhoods as well.)

The words *gracious* and *righteous* may sound as if they are in opposition to each other. We may think gracious means unconcerned about what's right and what's wrong. We may misunderstand righteous as meaning right and wrong are the only categories through which to view the world. But God is graciously righteous and righteously gracious.

God's grace is full of light, goodness, wellness, and, in this sense, righteousness. Grace is medicine that makes good living possible. And God's righteousness is not pinched, external, or starchy. God is simply *right* about what is good and true and beautiful. God's righteousness is full of compassion and kindness.

When I realize that grace and righteousness are integrated in the nature of God, I am able to join the psalm writer in saying, "Return to your rest, my soul, for the LORD has been good to you" (Psalm 116:7).

When my soul is restless, I can remind myself of how gracious God has been in my life. When my soul is restless, I can remind myself of how good and wise God is to lead me in the way that is just right for me. My soul's restlessness seems rooted in a vision of God as demanding something of me without empowering me to do it. What rest my soul finds when it trusts in the grace and goodness of God!

- *When you think about God as gracious and God as righteous, how do these sound to your ear? Do you sense resonance or dissonance within?*

- *Do they sound like different descriptions of God that don't easily come together? If so, talk with God about how your soul might rest in seeing them brought together. If not, give thanks to God for his gracious goodness and his good grace.*

7. A PLAYFUL GOD

*The Word became flesh and made his dwelling
among us. We have seen his glory, the glory of the one
and only Son, who came from the Father, full of grace
and truth. — John 1:14*

The eternal Son was born into human flesh and made himself at home among us. We saw his glory, a glory full of grace and truth. What a gift it is to have access to the Father through the Son who understands us and empathizes with us.

I had a unique experience of God-with-us one Easter morning. It was during a season when my tendency to self-accusation was especially strong. In such seasons, I carry in my gut a negative and untrue image of a God who lets me come to him but is mostly disappointed with my failures and shortcomings. I find it easy to talk with others about a Jesus who is joyful and gracious, but sometimes I struggle to remember this for myself.

When I rose to my alarm at five o'clock that morning, it was still dark. As I walked from my side of the bed to the master bathroom, I was careful not to wake my wife, Gem. Just before I reached the door, I heard a strong inner voice that said, "Ah, he is risen!" It had the same sound and feel as other times when I sensed the Spirit speaking to me. My first response was to think, *"He is risen" makes perfect sense on Easter. Christ is risen.*

Eventually, it dawned on me that perhaps God was being playful. He was using the familiar Easter language of resurrection to describe my getting out of bed. The voice didn't come with any tone of sarcasm or accusation. It sounded like the teasing of a friend. God seemed to be acknowledging me with affection and welcome.

But I had a hard time embracing this possibility and imagining Jesus being so playful on this day when we celebrate his resurrection. I was the one who should have said those words to him. But I came to experience that the new life of Jesus is playful, joyful, even lighthearted. "He is risen" is not just a historical fact but a living, breathing present reality. I am risen with Christ.

- *How does this little story strike you?*

- *How might the phrase "He is risen" be a meeting place for you and Jesus today?*

8. WHAT DELIGHTS GOD?

*He has no pleasure in the strength of a horse; nei-
ther does he delight in any[one's] strength. But
the LORD's delight is in those who fear him and
put their trust in his mercy. — Psalm 147:10–11
BCP2019*

It's easy to miss what this psalm is saying. It is not saying that
God despises horses or human strength that he himself created. Rather, the psalm is speaking of war horses and infantry
might. God is not impressed by our military resources that we
use to attack and defeat others. What pleases the Lord is not
what we accomplish with our resources and strength, but our
trusting, reverent orientation toward him.

Awaiting God's gracious favor is different from attacking to
get what we want using our own strengths and resources. In
today's world, people too often do the latter. But it's a delight-
ful thing to the heart of God when we humble ourselves, listen well, and follow him as closely as we can.

Reading the rest of Psalm 147, we hear a recitation of all God's initiatives and actions on behalf of his people: strengthening their protection, blessing their children, giving them peace with other nations, providing the best food, commanding the good of the earth, providing snow and rain, and so forth.

I wonder if a prayer like this one might arise in your heart as you reflect on these things: "Today, Lord, grant me a greater awareness of your initiative and your work, rather than being so impressed, obsessed, or even overwhelmed by my own work. Help me to remember that my work is small compared to yours. In helping me see this, cure me of empty pride and relieve me of the illusion that my yoke is heavier than it really is."

- *In what ways might you be tempted to focus on your own resources, capabilities, or strengths instead of cultivating a humble posture focused on God and entrusting yourself to the mercy of God?*

- *How might you acknowledge these things in the presence of God's mercy?*

9. MAKING A NAME, RECEIVING A NAME

Jesus' brothers said to him..."No one who wants to be-
*come a public figure acts in secret. Since you are doing
these things, show yourself to the world."...However,
after his brothers had left for the festival, he went
also, not publicly, but in secret. — John 7:3–4, 10*

Those who aspire to be public figures seek fame, reputation,
or recognition. Jesus' brothers assume this is what motivates
him—a name, visibility, popularity. They recommend he
show himself to the world at the Festival of Tabernacles in
Jerusalem. They assume Jesus wants the public spotlight, because that's their own motivation. Instead, Jesus prefers to go
to Jerusalem secretly.

How different from my personal instincts. Now that I have
written a few books, sometimes a desire arises in me to be a
public figure. There is a practical hope that more people will
read what I've written. But sometimes there is also a secret
hope that more people will admire or affirm me. Jesus, however, only wants to be seen and known as the Father would

reveal him to the world. He isn't looking to glorify himself but to glorify the Father who sent him.

This is actually freeing. Fame lacks meaningful substance. It comes and goes quite easily. I'm embarrassed at how strong my desire to be known can be. For example, I'm still tempted to base my sense of personal worth on whether people know me and value what I have to say.

I'm grateful, though, that the source of my worth never changes. My worth is still in who (and whose) I am. Writing books has not made me a different person. I am growing, but mostly I am the same person I was before I published anything. Popularity does not change who I really am. If I let the Father be the one to name me, then the names given me by the crowd hold less power over me.

- *In what ways are you (or have you been) tempted to seek your value in the opinions of others?*

- *A prayer like this may help you put this in perspective: "God, today give me an ear for the affirming voice and touch of blessing from you as Father, Son, and Spirit. Thank you that I am beloved not because of my accomplishments but because you have made me, chosen me, and are restoring me. Enable this to be my confidence today. Amen."*

10. POPULARITY AND PRIORITIES

But Jesus would not entrust himself to [the crowds],
for he knew all people. He did not need any testimony
about mankind, for he knew what was in each
person. — John 2:24–25

Many of us are hungry to be popular. We'd like more people to see our social media posts. We'd like more people to attend meetings we plan. We'd like more people to say good things about our life and work. But Jesus often did and said things to reduce his popularity. Listen to the words of Elton Trueblood about how Jesus related to the crowd:

> *It soon became obvious that Christ had no real hope in the crowds. They gathered, largely because of His reputation as a healer of diseases, often to gaze in wonder at a new and diverting sight. Their presence was no indication of a deep commitment. Consequently they could not be counted upon in a crisis. Crowds may be inevitable in a new redemptive movement, but it is not on the multitude that any movement can be built. Indeed, the passing popularity can be a*

*genuine barrier. Christ deliberately tried to limit His popularity by warning those whom He helped against making the help known.** *

So much about my experience of church has been focused on drawing a crowd and keeping them interested. This seems opposite the way of Jesus. This is because the crowds don't really know what they want. For example, they think they need excitement. But how much excitement is enough? The answer, generally, is a bit more than they experienced the last time.

And Trueblood's phrase that "passing popularity can be a genuine barrier" is especially telling. Our world lives by the idea that popularity is always good and that all press is good press. Jesus knew better. Popularity may be the fruit of our culturally held values, but not everything the crowds get excited about plays well with the values of God's kingdom. We may find that what drives popularity is actually going in the wrong direction.

- *What is your relationship to popularity these days? Are you hungry for it? Are you seeking it? Do you feel you do or don't have enough of it?*

- *How might the perspective of Jesus help you in dealing with your perceived popularity (or unpopularity)?*

* Elton Trueblood, Confronting Christ (New York: Harper, 1960), 20.

11. THE ANXIETY OF THE UNWELCOME UNEXPECTED

Can any one of you by worrying add a single hour to your life? — Matthew 6:27

I don't like surprises. I suppose there are exceptions, but my most common response to the unexpected is anxiety. I am still learning that surprises are not automatically threats. As I draft these words, I just got news that someone I was counting on for an upcoming shared event cannot join us. I felt that their contribution was key, and now I'll have to pick up that slack. My knee-jerk, unwilled reaction is worry.

But, Lord Jesus, you've said that anxiety does nothing to help me or my situation. You've said that worry will not add an inch to my stature or a day to my life. Anxiety does not enhance my life. It diminishes my life—my creativity, my vision, my joy, my hope, my energy. Anxiety is draining—even destructive.

So, when surprises jump out and startle me, I can do what you encouraged other worriers to do: focus my attention first on God's goodness and God's reign in my life and in my world. Unwelcome surprises cannot rob me of the faithful care and provision of God. That which overwhelms me in moments when I'm stunned by the unexpected is actually overwhelmed by the mighty, caring presence of God-with-us.

Instead of letting my autopilot anxiety response take the steering wheel of my will, and therefore my day, I can see my concerns against the backdrop of God's gracious, powerful, peaceful presence. God is bigger than unwelcome surprises.

- *How do you respond to unwelcome surprises? What happens in your thoughts, your emotions, even your body?*

- *To address this anxiety, take a moment to bring your worries into God's presence. Don't start by talking. Sometimes that just ends up rehearsing anxiety in front of God rather than bringing anxiety to offer to God. Be still and remember who God is and how God is with you. Let peace displace anxiety.*

12. EMPTY ENVY

Do not fret because of those who are evil or be envious
of those who do wrong; for like the grass they will
soon wither, like green plants they will soon die away.
Trust in the LORD and do good; dwell in the land
and enjoy safe pasture. Take delight in the LORD,
and he will give you the desires of your heart.
— Psalm 37:1–4

Do you ever fret because someone else is doing things wrong but apparently getting ahead? What if their bottom line is better than mine because of their unscrupulous and deceitful practices? Don't I have to follow suit if I am not going to be driven out of business? David addresses such concerns in Psalm 37. To paraphrase his words:

They are doing wrong, no question. And the results, for now,
are quite enviable. This worries you. I get it. But you're not
looking at a big enough picture. Your perspective is still small.
The day will come, sooner or later, when their wrongdoing
will be exposed and all that profit will come to nothing. They
aren't building anything that will last. Their profits are like

young grass in blistering weather that will wither almost as soon as it comes up. Take the long view of things.

What others gain through dishonesty and unscrupulous shortcuts is not lasting. Don't follow their way. Instead, trust in the Lord and his ways. Do what you know is right. You'll find that you're actually building something substantial and lasting if you do. Dishonesty is often more profitable for a season. The thief who takes cash from a local convenience store has a better hourly wage than most...for a time. But it's a wage that is on borrowed time. He lives without security. At any moment he can be caught, and his lucrative activity will catch up with him and bite him in the end. It's not a way to actually live.

And instead of delighting only in financial prosperity—which is a wonderful gift from the Lord and can be a great source of joy and gratitude—delight in the Lord himself. He is abundance personified. You'll find out that everything you really want is in him anyway.

- *When have you recently been tempted to envy? What did you think another had that you didn't?*

- *Why did you think their success was doing you harm? Talk with God about that.*

13. MATERIALISM: A SOUL ACCELERATOR

Jesus spoke to a wealthy person in the crowd: "Watch out! Be on your guard against all kinds of greed; life does not consist in an abundance of possessions."
— Luke 12:15

A good life, a rich life, an abundant life does not consist in having more material goods. But I live in a culture that is based on the assumption that this is exactly *how our lives get better....The drive to possess is an engine for hurry."**

Materialism makes our lives more hurried by defining the good life in terms of having more things. The pervading culture makes an implicit promise to us: buy more things and you'll have more joy (or peace or satisfaction or well-being). Having enough is surely better than living in poverty without even our basic needs met. But there comes a point when having more things just means having more worries, more unsatisfied desires, or more envy of those who *still* have more things than you do.

*Alan Fadling, *An Unhurried Life* (Downers Grove, IL:InterVarsity Press, 2013), 48.

Measuring the fullness of our lives by the abundance of our possessions is subject to the law of diminishing returns. The answer to the question, "How many things must I possess to be finally and fully satisfied?" is inevitably, "Just a little more than I have now." I believe I need more things to have more joy, so I must earn more money to buy those things. A hurried soul is one of the many taxes levied by a materialistic lifestyle.

What if I already have the most valuable abundance in the gift of communion with God through Christ? What if instead of frantically seeking abundance in outward ways, I could find contentment in the abundance that is already mine in God? What if I could live out of that abundance rather than living to get more of something I don't yet have?

- *What is your relationship with things like these days? Is there something that you've come to believe you must have to be really happy? What might that thing be?*

- *Can you envision experiencing joy now in the absence of that thing? Ask God to show you the way to embrace the life that is already yours.*

14. BREAKING BAD HABITS

No temptation has overtaken you except what is common to mankind. And God is faithful; he will not let you be tempted beyond what you can bear. But when you are tempted, he will also provide a way out so that you can endure it. — 1 Corinthians 10:13

In the case of habitual sin the choice of the will is confronted not only by the temptation of self-love but also by the strong force of habit; and if the sin is to be conquered the first step must be to break the habit. It is found by experience that the only way to do this is to lay the whole stress of direction at first on the lengthening of the intervals between the occasions of the sin. *

How are good habits formed? How are bad habits conquered? Reginald Somerset Ward offers some simple counsel for the latter question. Bad habits may not be easy to break, but his advice is straightforward: Lengthen the space between offens-

---

* Reginald Somerset Ward, A Guide for Spiritual Directors (London: A. R. Mowbray, 1957), 28.

es. It sounds a bit like the practical advice of recovery wisdom. Can you resist temptation today, in just this single moment? Of course. And when tomorrow becomes today and the next moment becomes the present, can you resist again? There will be grace for that moment.

We learn to live in the moment, to resist temptation in the moment, to practice the presence of God in this present moment. This moment is where grace is. This moment is where goodness is. Persistence in little, cumulative obediences makes a great deal of difference. This is the path of progress.

Ward's other bit of practical counsel is that we do not struggle alone. Again, this is recovery wisdom. Ward presumes that there is a relationship of spiritual direction in which one is learning to say those little, moment-to-moment nos. We have companions on the way to wholeness and holiness.

- *Is there a temptation that has become something of a bad habit of distance and dissipation in your life?*

- *With whom could you discuss this struggle? Who would listen and pray well with you? Who would be willing to walk alongside you as you learn to replace bad habits with holy habits? Ask God for guidance in this pursuit.*

15. THUNDERING HEARTS

At this my heart pounds and leaps from its place.
Listen! Listen to the roar of his voice, to the rum-
bling that comes from his mouth. He unleashes his
lightning beneath the whole heaven and sends it to
the ends of the earth. After that comes the sound of
his roar; he thunders with his majestic voice. When
his voice resounds, he holds nothing back. God's voice
thunders in marvelous ways; he does great things
beyond our understanding. — Job 37:1–5

These are the words of Elihu, the young friend who has listened to all the back-and-forth between Job and his three "comforters." Elihu speaks out of frustration with Job's complaining and his friends' inability to answer those complaints. I need to keep that context in mind when I read these words praising God. Everything Elihu says rings perfectly true. But he uses these words like a weapon against Job. Truth here is not in service of love.

There are moments when my own heart pounds and leaps from its place. There is emotional energy and resolve that rises up within me at times. I have moments when I genuinely feel interaction with God like that. Something stirs in me that feels alive, vital, and even heart-pounding. Can I believe there is something of the divine voice in such conversations that is causing my heart to leap within me?

But sometimes my heart seems disengaged. There is another part of me that resists, perhaps from fear. I find myself afraid of such passion, energy, and drive. That fearful part of me is childish, even adolescent. That part of me isn't growing whole and holy in Christ.

- *The following prayer may help you in your own transforming journey in the way of Christ: "May your voice thunder in marvelous ways today, Lord. May I hear the thunder. May I not resist your voice in fear. Let me hear your voice saying what you've said to so many others before me:* Do not be afraid. I am with you. *I'm grateful for this good news. Amen."*

16. TRANSFORMED THIRSTS

On the last and greatest day of the festival, Jesus stood and said in a loud voice, "Let anyone who is thirsty come to me and drink. Whoever believes in me, as Scripture has said, rivers of living water will flow from within them." — John 7:37–38

Jesus cries out and invites us to bring our thirsts to him. Just as Jesus invited the woman at the well to do in John 4, we could drink living water and never thirst again. In fact, instead of thirst, we would come to find rivers of living water flowing from within us—by which Jesus meant the fullness of God's Spirit flowing from within us. We could become not only temples (or vessels) of the Holy Spirit but conduits through which God's Spirit flows out into our relationships, our work, and our world.

The Greek phrase translated as "from within them" literally means "out of the belly"—the gut. Our places of deep feeling and passion can become profound expressions of the heart and passion of God's Spirit seeking to bring the world back to life in God through Christ. What we bring to God as a thirst could be transformed into a river. The key is to respond to Jesus' simple invitation, "Come to me. Trust in me. Drink of me." This is an invitation to stability, rootedness, and abundance.

- *Let this prayer become your own today: "Lord, I am thirsty, but I take my thirsts to places other than you. I take them to places of distraction, to self-indulgence, to ways of numbing, to empty amusement, to driven accomplishment. Show me how to bring my deepest thirsts to you today. Show me the path to being a person of abundance for the good of others. Amen."*

17. ALONE WITH GOD TOGETHER

Then, because so many people were coming and going that they did not even have a chance to eat, [Jesus] said to them, "Come with me by yourselves to a quiet place and get some rest." So they went away by themselves in a boat to a solitary place. — Mark 6:31–32

By themselves. A solitary place. Jesus invites his disciples to be alone together. Obviously they will be alone together *with Jesus,* but I also believe that alone *with God* is implied here.

I'm an introvert. I like to be alone. But this sense of being alone together with others happens less often in my life. I love opportunities when Gem and I can take a personal retreat together. We'll go to a nearby monastery and book two rooms. We are together over meals but alone with God the rest of the twenty-four hours.

I have led retreats where a majority of the time is spent alone with God but the attendees are in community together. I've been on eight-day silent retreats where I'm quiet before God in the presence of a few dozen others. We don't talk, even if we eat meals together at the same table. We are there together to be in the presence of God.

What are we doing? I believe we are responding to Jesus' invitation that he still extends today: "Come with me by yourselves to a quiet place and get some rest." Jesus takes the initiative ("come"). Jesus wants our company ("with me"). Jesus wants to curate moments for us to be alone with the Father as he himself has modeled ("by yourselves"). Jesus leads us, like the Good Shepherd he is, to a quiet place. Jesus gives us the gift of rest. Do you hear his words of invitation to you today?

- *What would it look like for you to follow Jesus to the quiet place where you can find rest in him for your soul? Talk with him about this.*

- *Schedule an appointment with Jesus into your upcoming calendar when you'll be able to accept his invitation.*

18. ENJOYING THE UNPLANNED TOGETHER

As for you, the anointing you received from him
remains in you, and you do not need anyone to teach
you. But as his anointing teaches you about all things
and as that anointing is real, not counterfeit—just as
it has taught you, remain in him. — 1 John 2:27

We are not desperately dependent on human teachers, but we can receive what God's Spirit wishes to teach us through them. Sometimes, however, we get caught up in our own ideas, our own opinions, our own plans. I love the way Thomas Merton speaks of such things in a letter he wrote to a friend who was coming to visit:

I look forward to seeing you and John H. and a few others in
October but let's make it purposeless and freewheeling and a
vacation for all and let the Holy Spirit suggest anything that
needs to be suggested. Let's be Quakers and the heck with
projects. I am so sick, fed up and ready to vomit with projects
and hopes and expectations.*

* Thomas Merton, The Hidden Ground of Love (New York: Farrar, Straus & Giroux, 1985), 83.

Merton looked forward to this informal visit by a few close friends to his monastery. Perhaps Merton suspected that his friends would feel pressure to "make the most of the time." Perhaps Merton was reacting to what he felt at the time was too much oppressive planning and projects in his particular monastic community. As a monk, Merton's life was fairly scheduled and left less time than he wished for purposeless freewheeling.

I am sometimes the one who saddles myself with a lot of plans and pressures. More recently, I've been learning to trust God's guidance of a meeting that I have some say in. Sometimes my tendency to be organized and structured has been about trying to control things rather than simply seeking to be responsible. Perhaps, like Merton, I'm becoming a bit more Quaker-like as I age.

- *Do you tend to be a more structured person or a more free-wheeling, spontaneous person?*

- *What happens when circumstances move against the direction of your preferred mode?*

- *How might such moments be opportunities to notice God's presence and discern God's guidance? Talk with God about this.*

19. HOPE ROOTED IN GOD

I hope in the Lord Jesus to send Timothy to you soon,
that I also may be cheered when I receive news about
you.... And I am confident in the Lord that I myself
will come soon. — Philippians 2:19, 24

Paul speaks to his friends in Philippi about his intentions and plans. Twice he speaks of these hopes as being "in the Lord Jesus." First, he says that he "hopes in the Lord Jesus" to send Timothy along soon to visit them. And then he speaks of being "confident in the Lord" that he himself will be able to come visit them in person.

Paul could certainly have said this more simply. Couldn't he have just told them, "I'm sending Timothy soon, and I expect to visit shortly as well"? Aren't we tempted to hear the other language as mere religious talk? But Paul isn't speaking empty words. Paul is expressing something dynamic and substantial about his life and his plans. He expresses his intentions and expectations, but he does so with abundant hope that Jesus will make his intentions fruitful. He has plans like the rest of us, but he has learned to walk closely with Jesus so that he has a strong sense of collaborative intention borne out of constant communion with the Lord.

Chuck Miller, a friend and mentor of mine, used to say that we should plan well but then hold our plans loosely. Planning is good, but we do not know the future. Jesus does. He may wish to guide our steps a bit differently than we had planned them. And so we make our plans in the Lord and we carry them out in communion with the Lord.

- *In what recent life situations have you made particular plans? How do you feel when your plans don't turn out the way you envisioned?*

- *How might you follow Paul's example and see your plans as a place of communion with Jesus and the implementing (or changing) of those plans as subject to the guidance of Jesus?*

20. WORKING IN GOD'S PRESENCE

Therefore, my dear brothers and sisters, stand firm.
Let nothing move you. Always give yourselves fully
to the work of the Lord, because you know that your
labor in the Lord is not in vain.
— 1 Corinthians 15:58

I may face many situations that make me feel shaky, but Paul encourages me to stand firm and unmoved. I have a secure place to stand in God. The kingdom of God is a place of stability and confidence for my soul. When feelings of anxiety, fear, self-doubt, or insecurity arise within me, they are not evidence that I'm no longer secure. I'm always safe in the presence of God.

I imagine Paul speaking personally to me: "Alan, keep giving yourself fully to the work the Lord has given you. Be confident that doing this work will not be empty effort." This brings focus to my work. I can learn to discern where my work is rooted in my own ideas and my own perspectives, and where I'm learning to work *with* Jesus. I pray, "Grant me wisdom in the midst of all the opportunities that arise each day. Help me see where you are working, what you are doing, so that I might join you there."

Because whatever work I do in communion with God will always be fruitful in the end, I can confidently and freely give myself to such work. The "work of the Lord" is available to me here and now. God is wanting to work in and through me in the context of my present job and my present relationships. May God's Spirit open our eyes to what he is wanting to do in and through us exactly where we find ourselves today.

- *Think about the work that lies ahead of you in the next twenty-four hours. How might those meetings, appointments, projects, or tasks be a place for you to work* with *God?*

- *How might people be helped or blessed? How might love be expressed? How might God's reign be shown more fully? Talk with God about this.*

PART 2: THE TRUTH OF GOD

21. GOD'S KINGDOM IS GOOD NEWS

Now after John was arrested, Jesus came to Galilee, proclaiming the good news of God, and saying, "The time is fulfilled, and the kingdom of God has come near; repent, and believe in the good news."
— Mark 1:14–15 NRSV

It won't come as a surprise to anyone reading this that the word *gospel* means "good news." What is the "good news of God" that Jesus is proclaiming? What makes it good? And to what degree does the good news that Jesus proclaims sound like the good news that is often proclaimed by North American Christians?

Jesus puts it simply: "The time is now. God's kingdom is near. Repent. Believe in this good news." The time is now and the kingdom is near because Jesus came into the world at a specific time and in a specific place. The kingdom is near *in him*. The good news is personal *in him*.

Jesus is close to us and we are close to him when we are following him and heeding his counsel, abiding in him in loving and humble obedience, and resisting impulses that take us away from him in empty acts. This is the spirit of his invitation to repent. It is both a turning away from and a turning toward. It's not just a matter of morality but a matter of loving allegiance to Jesus.

The good news for me today is that God's good reign is near me in Jesus. I can allow the good, pleasing, and perfect reign of God to hold sway in my life now. There is no better life. The impulses and desires that hold unbridled reign over so many don't lead to real goodness. The reign of God in our lives enriches and blesses us. The reign of unholy impulses and desires drains and damages us. The way of Jesus' reign in our lives really is good news. Let's turn ourselves to fully embrace it.

- *How would you describe what or even who rules your life today based on your priorities, values, and pursuits? Be as honest as you can.*

- *In what way might God be inviting you to turn away from something you're chasing so you can more fully trust and embrace his leadership in your life?*

22. THE SURPRISING GOOD NEWS OF REPENTANCE

And he said to them, "Thus it is written, that the Messiah is to suffer and to rise from the dead on the third day, and that repentance and forgiveness of sins is to be proclaimed in his name to all nations, beginning from Jerusalem." — Luke 24:46–47 NRSV

"Thus it is written." The writings of the Old Testament pointed ahead to a Messiah who, instead of coming as a heroic conqueror, would suffer and die. He would then rise on the third day to conquer an even greater enemy than Rome. He would conquer death. Here in Luke 24, Jesus is speaking to his inner circle after his resurrection. He is reminding them of what the Law, the Prophets, and the Writings had said about him.

The message that is to be proclaimed around the world in the light of this victory is one of repentance and forgiveness of sins in the name of Jesus. Forgiveness is good news. How good it is to know that God prefers to put our shortcomings and line-crossings behind him. God delights in mercy. He longs to forgive us more than we long to be forgiven.

But repentance is good news too. Many people assume that repentance is about limitations, legalism, or judgment. They assume it leads to a sour and pinched life. But repentance is good news because it says that necessary changes are actually possible. Aren't there realities about your present inner life that you would like to change? Aren't there ways you'd like to be more free, more whole, more fully healed and restored?

Repentance says that this freedom and healing are available if we turn toward the God who frees us and heals us. Repentance is turning away from that which harms us, enslaves us, and even poisons us. Repentance is turning our heart, mind, and body toward the One who heals, rescues, and restores us. Good news, right?

- *What is one way you desire for your inner life to change? Where are you hungry to be more free, more whole, more healed?*

- *What would it look like to turn toward the God who loves you and desires your freedom, wholeness, and healing even more than you do?*

23. THE GOSPEL IN WORD AND DEED

"There are people who say they do not need to make a vocal witness, because, as they express it, they 'just let their lives speak.' This appears as humility, but is really self-righteousness. No person's life is good enough to speak with any adequacy."[*]

This sounds a bit like the line attributed to Francis of Assisi: "Preach the gospel at all times. Use words if necessary." (By the way, there is no evidence that Francis actually said that.) Trueblood exposes the presumption that underlies such a statement. How will someone who knows nothing of the gospel figure out that our kindness, care, and goodness are fruits of communion with Christ without words that bear witness to this reality?

Of course, my way of life needs to harmonize with my verbal witness to the goodness, beauty, and truth of God's kingdom. But even at my best, the witness of my life alone doesn't say

* Elton Trueblood, Confronting Christ (New York: Harper, 1960), 12.

much about how the good that I do is the fruit of God's kingdom. The life of Jesus was perfectly good, but still he gladly proclaimed the good news of the kingdom in both word and deed. He invites us to bear witness to what we have seen and heard in him. Our lives can display the goodness and grace of his kingdom.

I certainly hope that my way of life will speak of the goodness and glory of Christ's work in and through me. But without words, there isn't a way for others to attribute that goodness to anyone but me. Acknowledging the fruitful work of Christ in me is an act of humility and worship. This requires words— good words, public words, praising words, thanking words.

- *Have you ever quoted that adage about preaching the Word and using words if needed? If so, how do you see that now?*

- *How would you like to speak about the goodness of what God has been doing in you so that others will understand and sense his invitation?*

24. A BIAS AGAINST JUDGMENT

For our sake he made him to be sin who knew no sin,
so that in him we might become the righteousness of
God. — 2 Corinthians 5:21 NRSV

"He [God] made him [Christ] to be sin." Christ, the one who was never guilty of any sin, was made to be sin. He identified himself with the sin that separated us from God so that we might actually become identified with God's righteousness. This is more than transactional language. This is *identity* language. Thanks to the generosity of Jesus, which I can fully trust, I am made welcome, right, and favored in God's eyes.

Far from coming to judge the world, Jesus came to identify with the core problem of the world and actually resolve it. To the Pharisees, who apparently had a habit of judging others, Jesus says, "You judge by human standards; I judge no one. Yet even if I do judge, my judgment is valid; for it is not I alone who judge, but I and the Father who sent me" (John 8:15–16 NRSV).

Don't we have the same habit? We tend to judge everything by our own human standards. I might expect Jesus to begin by saying something about how he judges differently, but Jesus prefers not to judge. That is not his preferred orientation or his main focus. But if the judgment of Jesus must come, it is true because it comes from perfect wisdom. God does not turn to judgment as a first response. His first response is loving care. If he judges, it is an expression of that care in the face of everything that dirties or distorts what he created good.

In your life, when you encounter Jesus and become aware of your own shortcomings and line-crossings, how do you imagine his posture toward you? Is he disappointed or is he compassionate? Does he cross his arms in displeasure or does he extend his arms in care? He comes to you, not to accuse but to heal, to restore, to forgive. What good news!

- *As you become aware of your own failings or disobediences, ask Jesus to reveal himself to you as one who identifies with your sins rather than one who stands apart to accuse or condemn. What does this do to your perspective? Your emotions?*

- *How do you wish to respond to this gracious Savior? Thanks? Praise? Petition?*

25. GOD OVERCOMES OUR ENEMIES

Praise be to the Lord, the God of Israel, because he has come to his people and redeemed them. He has raised up a horn of salvation for us in the house of his servant David (as he said through his holy prophets of long ago), salvation from our enemies and from the hand of all who hate us. — Luke 1:68–71

When the people of Israel in Jesus' day dreamed and prayed about God rescuing them, their focus was usually on the oppressive rule of Rome. They felt their lack of freedom under Roman authority, and they pleaded for God to overcome their enemy. That's the kind of salvation they were seeking from God.

I wonder if we're any different today. Aren't our prayers often focused on asking God to vanquish our outward enemies? We are in debt and want God to rescue us financially. We are in a difficult relationship and want God to change that other person. We are in a difficult job and want God to give us a new one. These are all perfectly reasonable prayers, and God cares about what concerns us.

But sometimes our greatest problems are not *out there* but *in here*. Sometimes our troubles are the fruit of something within us that we are unaware of. Enemies like anxiety, fear, anger, and lust do great harm to us and to those around us. So when God doesn't seem to answer our prayers about outward enemies, we fear that he isn't interested in them. But perhaps when God's saving activity seems to disregard what most concerns us, he is focused on something that will actually bring us a greater degree of true freedom. Sometimes God answers the prayers we don't know to pray.

God knows our true enemies better than we do. He knows that we are sometimes our own worst enemies, and he seeks to restore his kingdom purposes in our hearts.

- *What in your life recently has felt like an enemy "out there"? How would you like to talk with God about this?*

- *Are there any ways in which you have become a kind of enemy to yourself? How might the loving power of God be working to overcome this inner conflict? How might you cooperate with God's work?*

26. GOD CALLS US HIS OWN

Gilead is mine, Manasseh is mine; Ephraim is my helmet, Judah is my scepter. Moab is my washbasin, on Edom I toss my sandal; over Philistia I shout in triumph. — Psalm 108:8–9

Gilead was a region of the promised land east of the Jordan River that belonged to the tribe of Manasseh. Ephraim, Manasseh, and Judah are all tribes of Israel. These are the people of God, and in Psalm 108 God is saying that they belong to him.

What would it feel like to hear God say "You are mine" about the people who are dear to me or the places where I live my life? When it comes to my family, can I hear God saying, "Gem is mine, Sean is mine, Bryan is mine, and Chris is mine"? Can I imagine God saying "my helmet" and "my scepter" about those who are close to me? Through them God fights his battles and conducts his reign. They are intimately involved in the work of God. Amazing!

And then there are Moab, Edom, and Philistia, all enemies of Israel. God uses his enemies as a place to wash his hands, toss his sandals, and proclaim his victory. My enemies may feel overwhelming to me, but God sees them as insignificant.

So, just as I can have deep confidence that I belong to God, everyone and everything in my life also belongs to him. God is more concerned about what concerns me than I am. And those enemies that come against me are small and inconsequential in the presence of an Almighty God who happens to be my Father in heaven. When I let my concerns, worries, and fears loom large on the horizon of my emotions, imagination, or thoughts, I am forgetting this simple, potent, confident reality.

- *Think about the people or situations in your life. What would it feel like to hear God say to you, "This one is mine. That one is mine. These belong to me"? Take a moment to envision this.*

- *Now what about the enemies in your life—those things that oppose or challenge you? Can you imagine God treating these like a place to wash his hands, toss his sandals, and announce his victory? How does that feel?*

27. WORDS THAT RESURRECT

So they took away the stone. Then Jesus looked up and said, "Father, I thank you that you have heard me. I knew that you always hear me, but I said this for the benefit of the people standing here, that they may believe that you sent me." — John 11:41–42

This is the prayer Jesus prays just before speaking three words that display the resurrection power of God: "Lazarus, come out!" Jesus is grateful to the Father for hearing him. He isn't giving thanks for something unexpected. He is giving thanks for the sake of the crowd standing nearby. They need to trust the truth about Jesus, that he really has been sent by God to them...to us.

I feel awe as Jesus stands in front of Lazarus's tomb. Lazarus has been dead four days. In that climate, decay had already done its work in his body. But if Jesus can raise the dead by the power of God, he can reverse the effects of death in Lazarus's body. And he does.

Jesus speaks to the old and dead places in me, parts of my soul that did not know life. This is my journey to greater fullness for the sake of others. When I was a child, I had religious experiences without living knowledge of God-with-us. As a junior higher, I felt nothing of the affirming, treasuring love of the Father during those days of teasing and ridicule.

"Alan, come out!" Jesus says to those parts of me. "Come out of the tomb of self-accusation. Come out of the tomb of timidity and untruth. Come out of the tomb of hiding and avoiding. Step into the light." But this death has been at work far longer than four days. It's been years… decades. Even so, just as Jesus told the onlookers to unbind Lazarus and let him go (John 11:44), he says to me, "Come out! Be unbound and go free."

- *Where has it felt like death is at work in your perspectives, your viewpoint, your motives?*

- *Invite Jesus to speak the words that will bring life out of death within you. Why not ask him to do for your soul what he did for Lazarus's body.*

28. EMPTY PRAYERS, POWERFUL PRAYERS

Not to us, LORD, not to us but to your name be the
glory, because of your love and faithfulness.
— Psalm 115:1

Twice the psalmist says "Not to us." But we live in a culture that is most definitely glory-seeking. The singer here wants to remember that all true glory—all beauty and significance—finds its end in God. We don't have glory coming to us like the Lord does. The Lord is loving and faithful in ways we can't begin to be.

"Not to *me* today, but to *you* today, Lord. You are the weighty One. You are the shining One. You love me. I can count on you. And your love and faithfulness are both descriptions of how you treat those you have made, including me."

The singer goes on to unpack this glory perspective:

Why do the nations say, "Where is their God?" Our God is
in heaven; he does whatever pleases him. But their idols are

silver and gold, made by human hands. They have mouths, but cannot speak, eyes, but cannot see. They have ears, but cannot hear, noses, but cannot smell. They have hands, but cannot feel, feet, but cannot walk, nor can they utter a sound with their throats. Those who make them will be like them, and so will all who trust in them. (Psalm 115:2–8)

The culture around us takes God lightly but pours glory onto what amount to empty idols. There is so much empty glory in today's world. But idols cannot contain the glory we pour into them. They are a bottomless pit and a drain leading to nowhere. The "glory" of more money and possessions is no different from building an idol out of silver and gold. "Money, save me!" is a foolish prayer. "Fame, deliver me!" is empty. "Power, protect me!" will not bring me a single ounce of help when cancer or natural disaster or economic ruin strikes.

- *As you examine your own thoughts and intentions right now, how glorious is God in them?*

- *In what ways do you wish to notice God's glory and acknowledge it? Ask God's Spirit to give you eyes to see his beauty and his power in ways that provoke praise within you.*

29. HEALING, OR MERE RELIEF?

When Jesus saw him lying there and learned that he had been in this condition for a long time, he asked him, "Do you want to get well?" "Sir," the invalid replied, "I have no one to help me into the pool when the water is stirred. While I am trying to get in, someone else goes down ahead of me." Then Jesus said to him, "Get up! Pick up your mat and walk." At once the man was cured; he picked up his mat and walked.
— John 5:6–9

The paralyzed man in this passage had been by the healing pool for a long time and, in your own experience, maybe you understand something of how he must feel. In what way have you been disabled or unwell for a long time? Have you had— or do you now have—a specific idea about how you want God to heal you, free you, or restore you, but it hasn't happened yet? One reason we don't experience healing is implied in the question Jesus asks this man: *"Do you want to be made well?"*

We would expect that anyone paralyzed for thirty-eight years would of course want—desperately and passionately—to be made well, but some people have learned a way of life that accommodates their unwellness. In such cases, getting well could mean having to learn a completely different way of living. Also, sometimes the pain of change feels greater than the pain of staying the way we are. Sometimes we say we want healing or wholeness, but what we really want is relief or accommodation.

Finding relief usually means a temporary reprieve from what hurts. Being healed means being changed, and sometimes change hurts more in the short-term than the original pain. But the pathway of healing leads to a wellness and wholeness we never imagined was possible.

- *Is there some way in which you've needed healing of heart, mind, or soul for a long time now?*

- *Are you open to the painful but fruitful journey of healing? How are you tempted to stop at the request for relief alone?*

- *Talk to God about what these questions surface in you. If you find you want it, ask God to lead you into the work of deep transformation that leads to lasting change.*

30. RELIGIOUS IDEAS AND KINGDOM REALITY

*Meanwhile a large crowd of Jews found out that Jesus
was there and came, not only because of him but also
to see Lazarus, whom he had raised from the dead. So
the chief priests made plans to kill Lazarus as well, for
on account of him many of the Jews were going over to
Jesus and believing in him. — John 12:9–11*

Jesus raised Lazarus from the dead. Lazarus had been in the
tomb for four days, and there were countless witnesses who
knew he had actually died. In John 12, a crowd of Jews came to
investigate for themselves. But not all of those who came were
there to celebrate. Those in charge of the temple had a different response. They had no interest in the reality confronting
them but were only committed to defending their positions
and perspectives. Even in the face of an undeniable miracle,
they were stuck attacking reality to defend their beliefs.

The Jewish leaders refused to look into the claims of Jesus,
which were supported by the work (and works) he did. Instead, they felt compelled to protect their religious system and

their important place in it at any cost. This makes me think of something Elton Trueblood said:

> *"If Amos had waited for some authorization of his preaching, he would have waited forever and in vain. Entrenched privilege, whether civil or ecclesiastic, does not arrange easily for its own destruction. Sometimes the barren tree must be uprooted and the only one with the courage to uproot it is the person who has the boldness which arises from the direct sense of God's leading."**

"Entrenched privilege...does not arrange easily for its own destruction." But the chief priests were more interested in their religious power than they were in kingdom reality. Do we cling to beliefs at the expense of rejecting realities?

- *Can you see examples around you of people who cling to beliefs without regard to realities that confront them?*

- *Do you ever seek security in what you've understood to be true, even when those truths are called into question by something real that you've witnessed?*

- *Ask the Spirit of God to open your eyes to any ways in which you are more tempted to cling to beliefs about God than to God himself.*

---

* Elton Trueblood, Confronting Christ (New York: Harper, 1960), 114.

31. WALKING IN TRUTH OR WINNING ARGUMENTS

One day as Jesus was teaching the people in the temple courts and proclaiming the good news, the chief priests and the teachers of the law, together with the elders, came up to him. "Tell us by what authority you are doing these things," they said. "Who gave you this authority?" He replied, "I will also ask you a question. Tell me: John's baptism—was it from heaven, or of human origin?" They discussed it among themselves and said, "If we say, 'From heaven,' he will ask, 'Why didn't you believe him?' But if we say, 'Of human origin,' all the people will stone us, because they are persuaded that John was a prophet." So they answered, "We don't know where it was from." Jesus said, "Neither will I tell you by what authority I am doing these things." — Luke 20:1–8

This is one of many stories in the Gospels illustrating the conflict between Jesus and the Jewish leaders. Jesus came to announce truth—to describe reality. Apparently the Jewish leaders were more interested in being right than in being real. They wanted to win their argument more than they wanted to walk in truth. They didn't seem to care whether John was divinely sent or not. They had a position on the matter that they were now simply trying to prove.

What a dangerous place to find ourselves in! How many believe themselves to be engaged in the work of "defending the truth" but end up doing the same things as these Jewish leaders? Do some people win arguments at the cost of their own soul?

Father, may I always remain a learner in your presence. May I hold my arguments loosely so that I'm ready to be corrected or redirected by you. Protect me from defending my own positions or convictions when they conflict with divine reality. Amen.

- *Are you a person of strong convictions? In what ways or arenas?*

- *Are you learning the art of holding your convictions loosely enough to let Jesus counsel you and teach you? Talk to him about this.*

32. A FAITH JESUS DOESN'T WANT

But when Jesus turned and looked at his disciples, he rebuked Peter. "Get behind me, Satan!" he said. "You do not have in mind the concerns of God, but merely human concerns." — Mark 8:33

In Mark 8:32, Peter contradicts everything Jesus had just told the disciples about the Son of Man suffering and being rejected by the Jewish leaders before dying and rising again. Suffering, rejection, and death were not part of Peter's vision for what Messiah should experience. This was not a path to the sort of leadership he was hoping Jesus would exercise. He envisioned Messiah as a political and military leader against imperial Rome and religious Jerusalem.

Peter wants Jesus to win, but Jesus calls him "Satan," which means "adversary." I'm sure Peter saw himself on Jesus' side, but Jesus declares that Peter is against everything Messiah stands for. Peter's vision is merely human. He does not understand God's concerns.

This is where we get trapped. We often look at our lives, our families, or our work from a human perspective only. But as Christ followers we live and relate and work within the kingdom of God, which has a divine economy that functions differently from the without-God world in which we live. There is abundance rather than scarcity. There is selfless love rather than self-seeking individualism. There is holy hope rather than deep desperation. This is the kingdom Jesus sought first and Peter had overlooked.

When we pray, are we only bringing our concerns to God, expecting him to address them quickly and in the way we prefer? Or are we learning how to pray with the concerns of God in mind? When it comes to the person or situation I'm praying over, am I learning to ask what might be on God's heart here?

- *What or whom are you concerned about right now? What worries you, frightens you, or concerns you?*

- *Take a moment to ask God what is on his heart about this person or situation, and then be still and silent to see what God might do or say.*

33. EXPECTATIONS: WHEN JESUS LOOKS PAST OURS

When John, who was in prison, heard about the deeds of the Messiah, he sent his disciples to ask him, "Are you the one who is to come, or should we expect someone else?" Jesus replied, "Go back and report to John what you hear and see: The blind receive sight, the lame walk, those who have leprosy are cleansed, the deaf hear, the dead are raised, and the good news is proclaimed to the poor. Blessed is anyone who does not stumble on account of me." — Matthew 11:2–6

What is John asking for? John wants verbal confirmation that Jesus actually is the Messiah, or he wants Jesus to tell him to wait for someone else. Maybe John thinks Jesus is merely another forerunner of the actual Messiah, like himself. Perhaps John is looking for some sign that Jesus is going to deliver the Jews from Roman oppression. He hasn't seen any evidence of that yet.

What does Jesus give him in response? Jesus responds not with verbal affirmation but a declaration of visible evidence of the kingdom coming among those in need. He is a Messiah (King) who is doing the very things Isaiah said Messiah would do. But most people who were looking for Messiah had forgotten about the prophet's words. They expected ruling political power, but Jesus came in the power of kingdom compassion.

Since Jesus is not fulfilling the vision and understanding of the Jews (including John apparently) about the role of Messiah, they are offended.

We too can be quite attached to our expectations. Jesus reminds us that our expectations are not lord. He is.

- *When have you had expectations of Jesus that left you feeling disappointed?*

- *When did you want Jesus to say something, clarify something, change something, or do something and he didn't respond as you hoped or expected?*

- *How have you responded in the past? How would you like to respond now?*

34. JESUS AS LIGHT: BLIND OR SEEING?

Jesus said, "For judgment I have come into this world,
so that the blind will see and those who see will be-
come blind." — John 9:39

This story in John 9 is about a particular blind man whom Jesus healed. Listen to what the man says to the religious leaders who claim to see: "He answered, 'I have told you already and you did not listen. Why do you want to hear it again? Do you want to become his disciples too?' Then they hurled insults at him and said, 'You are this fellow's disciple! We are disciples of Moses!'" (John 9:27–28).

The blind man who now sees chides the Jewish leaders who are actually still blind. This man, who had learned to live in the midst of a hard reality and now has found profound freedom, has a unique vantage point on just how trapped these Jewish leaders really are. I hear sarcasm as he asks them, "Do you also (like me) want to become his followers?" They are furious at such an impertinent question, but this only serves to expose how blind they are to what they are witnessing. A blind man now sees, but they are arguing about other things.

Jesus didn't come to condemn, but he did come to expose. Jesus is the light, and wherever Jesus goes he brings everything into light. But how rarely do we see things as they actually are. Jesus came as a light to enlighten everyone who is willing to see. Some people claim to see but are actually blind. Others know they are blind but long to gain their sight.

- *In what ways do I mistakenly assume I already see things as they are?*

- *In what ways do I know I am blind but ready to be given sight?*

- *What does it look like for the blind man to actually see, not just with physical eyes but with eyes of the heart?*

35. SEEING JESUS, WORSHIPING JESUS

Jesus said, "You have now seen him; in fact, he is the one speaking with you." Then the man said, "Lord, I believe," and he worshiped him. — John 9:37–38

As in the previous chapter, we're considering the story of the blind man healed by Jesus. The man asks Jesus, "Who is he [i.e., the Son of Man], sir? Tell me so that I may believe in him" (John 9:36). Our focus verses contain Jesus' answer to that question. The blind man knows that he's been healed, but he does not yet know the true identity of the one who has healed him. We will often see kingdom benefits before we gain kingdom understanding. Grace often precedes (and enables) knowledge.

When it comes to our inner sight—something the Jewish leaders simply didn't have and so remained inwardly blind—being *able* to see may not be as important as *who* we see. We need the Spirit of God to open the eyes of our heart so that we see Jesus in his love, his grace, his power, his wisdom, his goodness. He is the one speaking with us. He is the one inviting us to trust him and to express our perception of his worth with words of worship. He wants us to see and respond to the reality of who he is. We need this more than he needs this.

- Offer a prayer to Jesus in the spirit of this one: *"Lord, today I believe. You took a blind man and gave him spiritual sight. I was utterly blind to you, to your kingdom, and to your good and living way, but you drew me to the Father. I believe you and am learning to trust you more. You are so good, so beautiful, so right, so wise, so kind, so gracious, so gentle, so humble. My heart is filled with reverence, gratitude, humility, love, and joy. I feel it like a warmth in my chest and a tear in my eye. Thank you for your Spirit who enables me to dwell in your presence throughout this day in everything I do and everyone I'm with. Amen!"*

36. AT HOME IN TRUTH AND LOVE

The elder, to the lady chosen by God and to her children, whom I love in the truth—and not I only, but also all who know the truth—because of the truth, which lives in us and will be with us forever: Grace, mercy and peace from God the Father and from Jesus Christ, the Father's Son, will be with us in truth and love. — 2 John 1–3

The apostle John has much to say about truth here, but John is not talking about truth in the sense of historically rooted systematic theology, or right beliefs about God, or anything of a merely cognitive, intellectual bent. He is talking about spiritual reality in Christ.

I love someone in the truth when my relationship with them more and more corresponds to the reality of God's kingdom in which grace, mercy, and peace are the reigning orientation. *That* is reality. Knowing the truth is not merely knowing about God. As James says, even demons know about God (James

2:19). Knowing the truth is having a heart, mind, soul, and body that are increasingly in harmony with kingdom reality.

Jesus, I'm grateful for the places of deeper spiritual reality into which your Spirit has enabled me to walk over my lifetime. Too often, I have been satisfied with a vision of truth that is more "about" than "of" or "in." Now I am seeing myself more truly, even in my shortcomings. I am learning to face my weaknesses like an adult rather than like a scared child or an insecure adolescent. I love how good this is. I want to walk in truth—in reality—today. Help me do just that, Jesus. Amen.

- *What kingdom reality has Jesus been trying to help you see most recently?*

- *What is true in the presence of God that you need to grow more confident in? Talk with God about this.*

37. TRUTH DEFINED BY LOVE

And this is love: that we walk in obedience to his commands. As you have heard from the beginning, his command is that you walk in love. I say this because many deceivers, who do not acknowledge Jesus Christ as coming in the flesh, have gone out into the world. Any such person is the deceiver and the antichrist.

— 2 John 6–7

I remember hearing a lot about the antichrist as a young believer. I came to faith in a church that majored on preaching about the end times and all kinds of apocalyptic themes. It's taken a while, for example, for me to recover my love for the book of Revelation.

But hear what John says about the kind of person who is a deceiver and antichrist: it is the person who denies that Christ actually came in the flesh. Perhaps more important, it is the person who does not walk in obedience to what Christ commands. The person who fails to walk in love. The simplest operating definition of what it means to be "anti-Christ" is to be disobedient and unloving.

If we claim to be followers of Jesus, then the clearest evidence of that is living in the way of Jesus and seeking to follow Christ's example of obedience to his Father. Obedience is simply a way of staying put in the love of God—of receiving his love and showing his love to others. Love is the greatest command. Love is the surest sign that we are living our lives in Christ, wherever he has planted us.

The command of Jesus is that we walk in love, especially in relation to one another. It is in this light that I can recognize the nature of those deceivers who deny Christ's incarnation to be among us. They do not walk in love. They seek self-defined, self-serving outcomes.

- *We do not want to be like those who live counter to the purposes and ways of Christ. How is Christ inviting you to join him in his intention to love the world through you today?*

- *How might you live in line with Christ's command to love? Think of a specific next step you can take today.*

38. LEADERSHIP: RECEIVING AND GIVING GOOD

I will exalt you, LORD, for you lifted me out of the depths and did not let my enemies gloat over me. LORD my God, I called to you for help, and you healed me. — Psalm 30:1–2

Here David expresses his intention to exalt the Lord. Why? What inspires him? He tells us, "For you lifted me out of the depths and did not let my enemies gloat over me." David experiences God's Spirit lifting him from the deep place in which he finds himself. Was it depression? Despair? Discouragement? Whatever the dark place was for David, the Lord lifted him out of it. Whoever or whatever sought David's harm and put him in that pit is overcome by the God of the universe.

When I read those first two lines, in my heart I hear something like, "How could I help but exalt you, Lord, when you have first exalted me?" It sounds like an echo of the words of John in his first letter—"We love because he first loved us" (1

John 4:19)—but with *exalt* in place of *love*. I think it works just as well.

How do I respond when I find myself in a deep, dark place? Do I hang my head and stare into the darkness? Or am I learning to follow David's good way of looking for God and crying out for his help? When we look up, we'll find that God continues to be a Good Shepherd to us. Our cry for help is met with his gracious healing touch in our lives. The time between cry and healing may not be instantaneous, but God's faithfulness will be at work to bring healing in his time.

Whatever we offer God or give to another is always something we've first been given by God. An expression of true joy is an overflow of the joyful heart of the Father, Son, and Spirit in whom we live and move and have our being. As we learn to not be anxious for anything, we experience the fruit of God's peaceful presence in ourselves and among one another.

- *Are you now or have you recently found yourself in a dark place?*

- *What would it be like to look up and cry to God for help? How might you do that now or soon?*

39. GOD'S GOOD JUDGMENT

I do not shrink from your judgments, because you yourself have taught me. — Psalm 119:102 BCP

When I read the word *judgments*, my first reaction is to assume that the psalmist is talking about condemning judgment. I imagine God sitting on a throne of accusation. Who wouldn't shrink from condemnation by an all-knowing God? Instead, the psalmist is speaking of judgment in terms of God's declarations about reality. The psalmist is inviting us to embrace how God tells us exactly the way things are. When God speaks, his words describe reality.

We can let go of the belief that God's main purpose is to accuse and condemn us. God did not send Jesus into the world to condemn the world but to save it (John 3:17). In Christ, there is absolutely no condemnation for us, because God's Spirit has set us free from the reign of sin and death in us (Romans 8:1–2).

When God speaks reality to me, even if it seems unpleasant in the moment, it is always good. I learn from God. I see my fantasies and bent perspectives in the light of what actually is. I learn to trust his assessment of my life. He intends my good. In that way, the judgments of God are *always* good news. Rather than shrinking from the declarations of God, I'm learning to lean into this sort of divine counsel.

- *Can you think of something in your life, past or present, that you may be tempted to hide from God's sight, perhaps for fear that you would be condemned?*

- *Imagine instead a vision of the God who comes to forgive, to heal, to restore that very place in your life. How might this change your perspective and your approach to God?*

- *Why not take a few moments to pray your own version of our focus verse from Psalm 119? Perhaps it would sound something like this: "Lord, I want to stop hiding from you. I can't hide from you, even when I try. And being seen by you is like being seen by the wisest healer, counselor, or friend I could imagine. See me now. Heal me now. Guide my steps now. Amen."*

40. THE WISDOM OF LOVING GOD

I am writing to you, fathers, because you know him who is from the beginning. — 1 John 2:13a

The best spiritual fathers are the ones who are most mature, who are eldest among us, who are most responsible for others. John has a message for these fathers because they are the ones who know the eternal God. John does not acknowledge them for their business success or their personal impressiveness. He speaks to them because they know God.

Spiritual fathers are those who have learned that anything that disregards the God who created this world is making empty promises. This is how John puts it: "For everything in the world—the lust of the flesh, the lust of the eyes, and the pride of life—comes not from the Father but from the world. The world and its desires pass away, but whoever does the will of God lives forever" (1 John 2:16–17).

Spiritual fathers are those who recognize that what this world promotes as high value is temporary and short-lived. Fathers are those who have an unhurried vision of goodness and priorities. Young men and women in the kingdom are those who spend their lives seeking out and satisfying bodily cravings and self-promoting visions of personal success.

"Do not love the world or anything in the world. If anyone loves the world, love for the Father is not in them." (1 John 2:15)

Fathers and mothers in the faith have learned that seeking life in the promises of this world and seeking life in God are two different paths. John isn't saying that I shouldn't have a great affection for the beauty and goodness of what God has made. In this verse, "world" refers to a universe that has decided to seek life apart from the living God. It has always been an empty and futile pursuit, but it has captured many people's imaginations. May I continue on the path toward becoming a mature parent in the kingdom of heaven.

- *Where do you find yourself on your journey of loving and trusting God?*

- *Are you young in the faith and so growing through spiritual childhood? Are you a young adult in the faith, learning to distinguish the difference between allowable and excellent, and embracing the latter? Or might you be growing up into spiritual parenthood? Talk with God a bit about these things.*

PART 3: THE LIFE OF GOD

41. DEATH AND RESURRECTION: HOW THE KINGDOM WORKS

So will it be with the resurrection of the dead. The body that is sown is perishable, it is raised imperishable; it is sown in dishonor, it is raised in glory; it is sown in weakness, it is raised in power; it is sown a natural body, it is raised a spiritual body.
— *1 Corinthians 15:42–44*

Resurrection is central to our experience of God. It is a key cornerstone of our living faith and our growing trust. In my Anglican tradition, we remember together that "I believe in... the resurrection of the body and the life everlasting." The death of our bodies is not the end of our existence, regardless of what some people think these days. Our physical bodies will indeed die and be buried like a seed.

That perishable body is raised imperishable—a never-dying body at home in the kingdom of heaven. A decaying body is raised a glorious body. That weak body is raised in and with power. That natural body will grow like a seed into a spiritual body.

What you sow does not come to life unless it dies. When you sow, you do not plant the body that will be, but just a seed, perhaps of wheat or of something else. But God gives it a body as he has determined, and to each kind of seed he gives its own body. (1 Corinthians 15:36–38)

I've learned that the first thing a seed does after it is planted is grow roots. Roots precede shoots. This is how our lives work. If we want our lives to be fruitful and productive, death will precede life—resurrection life. Life begins with roots—invisible life, foundational life, the beginnings of sustainable life.

While I like this as a theory, I never seem to like when some part of me, or some dream or plan or vision, has to die. I assume that this is the end of it. But that is not how God's kingdom works. The death of anything is the first step in a different kind of life—an eternal kind of life. This requires patience and humility.

- *In what ways have you experienced something that felt more like death than life in your journey so far?*

- *Have you begun to see anything that looks like resurrection from that place of death? This might be a good conversation to have with God.*

42. THE GRACE OF A STEADFAST HEART

My heart, O God, is steadfast; I will sing and make
music with all my soul. — Psalm 108:1

I love the image of David's steadfast heart. When my heart is distracted or unsteady or timid, I can find, like David did, a heart that is confident, stable, even steadfast. How does that happen? What would that look like? I find that a good place to start is by opening my heart and pouring out what is in it before God. I talk with God honestly about the thoughts and feelings that are present in my mind and heart.

But then, like David, I often find myself rehearsing the reality of God. I acknowledge the grandeur of God above all my puny little thoughts and feelings. I ask for what I need: salvation and help. Listen to David's way of doing this:

> *For great is your love, higher than the heavens; your faithful-*
> *ness reaches to the skies. Be exalted, O God, above the heav-*
> *ens; let your glory be over all the earth. Save us and help us*

with your right hand, that those you love may be delivered.
(Psalm 108:4–6)

David's prayer inspires one in me: "O God, your love for me—for us—is so vast that it reaches higher than the sun, the moon, and the stars. Yours is no small love. And your faithfulness—your reliable, powerful availability to me—is greater than the atmosphere above me and the clouds in the sky today. Be exalted, O God, in my life and work today. May who you are and what you do be the largest reality for me. May the beauty and weightiness of who you are fill me and overflow me as I write or work or speak or whatever I may do. *Amen.*"

- *What are some of the words you would use to describe the condition of your heart today?*

- *What positive or negative words capture this reality for you? Reflect on this in the presence of the God whose love and faithfulness is measureless.*

- *What words do you want to say to God about whatever need for rescue or help you may have in this season?*

43. THE TEMPLE OF OUR BODIES

But the temple [Jesus] had spoken of was his body.
— John 2:21

When Jesus said, "Destroy this temple, and in three days I will raise it up" (John 2:19 NRSV), he was speaking about his own body as a temple—and the Jews misunderstood. They heard him speak these words while standing in *the* temple—the Jerusalem temple. Jesus, however, understood his own body to be a place of worship, of offering, of presence.

What would happen if I had a clearer vision of my own body as a temple for the Lord? How might my moments be transformed if I remained awake to God *with* me and God *in* me? How might that awareness change how I work, how I relate to others, even how I eat? My physical disciplines tend to rise and fall with my sense of God-with-us and of who this God-with-us is.

Trusting the goodness of the God who is with me would enable me to experience the abundance such a good God gives.

Fear rooted in a distorted image of God will keep me far from God and far from the actual goodness of God's presence.

So what prompted Jesus to speak about his body as a temple? The sign of authority Jesus offered to the Jews was a cryptic comment about his coming death and resurrection. Jesus knew it was coming; his disciples did not.

My heart rises with this prayer: "Jesus, you understood your body to be a temple: you were aware that the Holy Spirit fully indwelled you as you went about preaching, healing, and caring for people. I understand that the same is true of me as I live in you and you live in me. I have not always treated my body like a temple as you did yours. I want to follow your way in this. Strengthen my mind, my will, and my body to this end. Amen."

- *In what ways does your knowledge of your future death and resurrection impact how you live in your body now?*

- *Since you are actually raised with Christ already, what impact does that have as you, a risen one, walk through your day?*

- *How might you entrust yourself to God's abundance and be available today to be blessed by God and be a blessing to others?*

44. INVITING GOD'S GUIDANCE

The mind governed by the flesh is death, but the mind governed by the Spirit is life and peace. The mind governed by the flesh is hostile to God; it does not submit to God's law, nor can it do so. — Romans 8:6–7

I feel sad for the ways I still allow my mind to be fixated on and steered by desires that are not sourced in the life of God. Pursuing pleasures, or escaping from reality, or chasing recognition from others does not lead me to life but to death, not to peace with God but to conflict with God and his way for me. Why do I still allow myself to be driven by such empty thoughts?

Paul uses the word *govern* here to help me understand. When I allow my desires apart from God to direct and manage my life, I find life draining from me rather than constantly renewing me. When I allow my surface desires, which are often twisted or hijacked by so many different voices out there, to dominate my decisions and actions, that surface turbulence distracts me from my truer and deeper desires in God.

I wonder what all this might sound like as a personal invitation from God.

"Alan, living according to the flesh means you've set your mind on desires apart from me. If you live in accordance with my Spirit, you set your mind on what I desire. You can discern what is ruling you by whether you find yourself experiencing life or death, peace or inner resistance. Let me rule your mind and so rule your life. You'll find you're able to live according to my guidance and in my way. And you'll find it to be a path of life."

- *Where in your life are you experiencing a certain resistance to God and God's ways? What is that producing in your day-to-day life?*

- *How would you like to invite God to give direction—to govern—your life in these places? If God's voice were to come now, what might that invitation to trust and follow sound like?*

45. FORGIVEN LITTLE, LOVING LITTLE

Therefore, I tell you, her sins, which were many, have been forgiven; hence she has shown great love. But the one to whom little is forgiven, loves little.
— *Luke 7:47 NRSV*

In Luke 7, Jesus doesn't deny that this woman who has washed his feet with her tears and dried them with her hair has a notorious reputation. He even says that her sins are many. But is Jesus really saying that some people need forgiveness for greater amounts of sin and other (good) people (like us?) have nearly no sin at all? I wonder if Jesus' statement is more a matter of awareness than it is of quantity.

We all fall short in countless ways. The Pharisees were quick to see sin in the lives of others and quick to put a holy face on themselves for anyone who was looking. They failed to see the sins, which were many, in their whitewashed hearts. They did not realize their own need for forgiveness.

And then Jesus makes this remarkable equation: the more we understand ourselves to be forgiven, the more love we embrace and share with others. If I feel that I have hardly anything to be forgiven, I will have little gratitude, little humility, and little care for others. I will tend to judge others rather than love them. But when I realize just how deep and wide is the mercy that I myself have needed, then I have a fullness of mercy that overflows toward others in their need for forgiveness.

Jesus says that this woman's kisses and anointing showed him more love and honor than the Pharisee host had shown him. No other Jewish leader would have seen it that way. What the Pharisee surely saw as dishonoring, Jesus saw as honoring. What the Pharisee saw as polluting, Jesus saw as blessing. This is Jesus' way of truth, mercy, and love.

- *When are you tempted to judge another? What is it that tempts you to look down on them?*

- *Might this be the very place where you yourself need to receive the mercy of Jesus in your own life? Why not take a few moments to reflect on this idea prayerfully.*

46. THE EMPOWERING MOTIVE OF COMPASSION

So they went away by themselves in a boat to a solitary place. But many who saw them leaving recognized them and ran on foot from all the towns and got there ahead of them. When Jesus landed and saw a large crowd, he had compassion on them, because they were like sheep without a shepherd. So he began teaching them many things. — Mark 6:32–34

Jesus and his disciples take action to obey his words of invitation: "Come with me by yourselves to a quiet place and get some rest." But while they are in the boat on their way, a crowd runs ahead of them and meets them on the other shore. When Jesus sees them, his emphasis on the importance of rest is superseded by his shepherd's heart for the crowd.

Jesus often rose each morning before anyone else to get away and be alone in the presence of the Father. Apparently sometimes he also stayed up later than everyone else to do the same. But, at least in this case, compassion trumps his plans to withdraw. Sometimes the need of the moment supersedes my own needs.

But if I never withdraw to the lonely places, if I always defer to the needs of others and make myself always available, I may find that I don't have much to offer them. I must learn how to keep the cup of my life full to overflowing so that I can fruitfully serve those who cross my path.

Jesus, the Good Shepherd, is moved to service by the needs he sees in the crowd. We are his followers. As we witness the priorities of Jesus, they can become our priorities as well. And we can remember that Jesus still continued to withdraw to lonely places to pray. There is a holy and dynamic tension between solitude and community, between prayer and ministry, between contemplation and action. May God's Spirit be the one to guide us as we navigate that tension.

- *How would you describe the relationship between solitude and ministry in your life these days? Does one get more attention and energy than the other?*

- *How might Jesus be inviting you to follow his rhythm in these things as you reflect on your life and work in this season?*

47. BECOMING SPIRITUAL ADULTS

You have taken off your old self with its practices and
have put on the new self, which is being renewed in
knowledge in the image of its Creator.
— *Colossians 3:9–10*

I've sometimes imagined that my old self that needs to be put off is a child or adolescent, and that the new self is a mature adult. Below, I've paraphrased Colossians 3:1–11 with this perspective in mind.

Since I am a mature man who has been raised with Christ, I must set my heart on higher things. This is where Jesus Christ is. It's a place of honor and favor at God's right hand. I can learn to set my mind on higher things instead of base things. That childish way of life is past—as good as dead. It no longer exists. My real life—my mature adult life—is actually hidden with Christ in God. And since Christ really is my life, then I will be where he is—now and in future glory. So it makes sense to put to death whatever has its roots in that old and juvenile way of life: misuse of sex in every way, every desire that leads me away from abiding in God, and idolatrous greed. This is the stuff that provokes God's anger. I used to live this way when I didn't know any better, but now I really must get rid of everything that grows out of anger, evil intent, hurtful or dirty words. Lies are never helpful, since they are rooted in that old and dead way, which I've taken off, and are completely out of place with the new self, which is always being made new again in contemplating and knowing my Creator. In this new life, all merely human distinctions are meaningless—Gentile or Jew, circumcised or uncircumcised, barbarian, terrorist, slave or free. Christ is everything and is in everything.

- *Was there a line that seemed to especially hit home? Why?*

- *How would you like to interact with Jesus about that?*

48. PEACE OR CONFLICT WITH GOD?

Those who live according to the flesh have their minds set on what the flesh desires; but those who live in accordance with the Spirit have their minds set on what the Spirit desires. — Romans 8:5

This conflict between flesh and Spirit hits closer to home for me the longer I live. I find myself on either side of this tension at different points in my life, my week, even moment-to-moment. I am letting my flesh steer my life when I wander into places where my awareness of and allegiance to God's real presence, God's abundant goodness, and God's faithfulness wanes.

In such places I find myself driven by longings for pleasure, power, or position. I begin to believe that the peace I thirst for will come from something out there that I do not yet have. I imagine there is something somewhere else that will somehow fill the vast space of my soul here and now. That's the empty promise my flesh leads me to pursue.

At other times, I can and do set my mind on what the Spirit desires, which is eternal and alive and beautiful. This is a way of life and peace rather than a way hostile to God and God's kingdom. The Spirit reminds me that only God can satisfy my deep longings. When I remember God-with-us and who God is with me, I find my mind and heart more alive and secure. I find myself at home in the good, pleasing, and well-fitting purposes of God. Instead of being resistant, I am receptive to eternal life.

When I allow my mind to be ruled by desires that distance me from God-with-us, obviously I cannot submit to God. And I cannot satisfy apart-from-God desires from a place of abiding in God—not *shouldn't*, but *can't*.

- *In what ways have you found yourself resistant to the life God is inviting you to? What would you like to say to God about such moments or seasons?*

- *In what ways do you find yourself drawn closer to the God whose Spirit gives life? How would you like to draw nearer now?*

49. BATTLING INTERNAL ENEMIES

O LORD, how many are my foes! Many are rising against me; many are saying to me, "There is no help for you in God." But you, O LORD, are a shield around me, my glory, and the one who lifts up my head. I cry aloud to the LORD, and he answers me from his holy hill. — Psalm 3:1–4 NRSV

One of my continual battles is the one that happens in my own heart and mind. I continue to discover and fight negative patterns of thought and emotion that are shaped less by Jesus and more by the world around me. The words of David's psalm ring true for me.

The enemies David mentions are human, probably military. Like his enemies, my negative thoughts and emotions insinuate that I'll be finding no help from God. Such thoughts and emotions pester me and hound me. They rise against me. They whisper that I am abandoned and alone. They oppose everything good that God intends for me.

So I'm grateful when I am awake enough to respond as David does with a hearty "But you, O Lord are..." What is God? He is my shield. He surrounds me with protection. He is my glory. He makes my life shine so that it has impact. He is the one who lifts my head. He encourages my soul in the face of discouragement or accusation.

When I feel surrounded by trouble, like David I can cry out to the Lord. He answers my cry with holy help. He is my strong friend when the thoughts in my heart and head feel like enemies.

- *In what ways do your thoughts or feelings sometimes feel like enemies? Take a moment to write about some of those internal adversaries. Name them.*

- *Now take a moment to cry out to the God who is with you to help you. How might he desire to help you against these particular enemies?*

50. THE UNHOLY NARROWS

*Enter through the narrow gate. For wide is the gate
and broad is the road that leads to destruction, and
many enter through it. But small is the gate and narrow the road that leads to life, and only a few find it.*
— *Matthew 7:13–14*

I'm amazed at those who assume that the small gate and the
narrow road coincide with their small, narrow ideas about
God and God's ways. To me, their definition of narrow does
not look like an abundant life. They seem more often to live
pinched, cramped lives, with little joy, peace, or love, and a lot
of anger and judgment.

A person can live in a narrow way that is empty of life and full
of destruction. The reason few people find the narrow way of
God's kingdom has nothing to do with whether they attend a
particular church or participate in a particular denomination.
They don't find it because they don't actually want to surrender and fully entrust themselves to the mystery and majesty
of who God is. They want a God they have full control over,

a God who fits in their tiny box with its narrow definitions, a God they think they understand perfectly. These are the unholy narrows.

The narrow way that Jesus defines will challenge *everyone*. We will experience a certain discomfort when we encounter that way. It will squeeze out of us everything that is *not* life. It will squeeze out pride, conceit, self-satisfaction, and judgment of others. If I feel comfortable with my own definition of narrow, then likely I have missed its true meaning.

- *What has it looked like for you to encounter the narrow way of Jesus?*

- *In what ways has that narrow way challenged you and drawn you to places of surrender? In what ways have you been tempted to define narrow that made you feel more comfortable?*

- *What do you sense Jesus is saying to you in all of this?*

51. DEATH DOESN'T WIN

The sting of death is sin, and the power of sin is the
law. But thanks be to God! He gives us the victory
through our Lord Jesus Christ.
— *1 Corinthians 15:56–57*

If death were a bee, its sting would be sin. If the law were part of a human body, it would be the muscular system. What does this mean?

Let's think about the idea of sin as separation or disconnection, like a branch detached from a vine. When a loved one dies, our separation from them stings. For those of us who hope in eternal life through Christ, death stings less, but it still stings.

As a system of restrictions or imperatives, the law is what gives power to the separation of sin. Up against any unbending law, I realize my weakness and frailty. I see how imperfectly I abide in the One who gives life.

Thankfully, the truth about sin as sting and law as power gets reversed in verse 57 with the simple conjunction "But..." Those things are true about death and sin, *but* that is not the end of the story. Our risen Lord Jesus Christ has triumphed over these dynamics of sin, death, and law, and has graciously given us the gift of life. Life is an engine that overcomes death's sting of sin and sin's power in the law.

I am being offered the reality of the comfort and freedom of the life of God in the risen Christ. I am free from the sting of being separated from God. I am free from the ways in which law empowers sin. I am free to live in relationship with God rather than trying to perform for God.

- *What in your life seems to sting these days? What feels like it has power over you?*

- *How might the life and grace of Jesus meet you right in these places to bring freedom and comfort? Talk to him about this.*

52. A GOOD DEATH

And if the Spirit of him who raised Jesus from the
dead is living in you, he who raised Christ from the
dead will also give life to your mortal bodies because
of his Spirit who lives in you. — Romans 8:11

As I write this, I am entering the last year of my fifties. I have been feeling the reality of my body's mortality in ways I didn't in my thirties or forties. Back then, mortality was about the last thing on my mind. Now, I find myself reflecting on this reality. I am more aware now that this body will not live forever, even as I trust that I will live in God's kingdom forever.

But this mortal body that is dying is indwelt by the Spirit who raised Jesus from the dead. The death of my mortal body, while it is closer now than ever before, is not the biggest reality about me. For the Spirit of resurrection dwells in this body.

I'm not trying to be morbid. In fact, when I was on retreat at a nearby monastery, I remember hearing monks in their compline prayers closing out the day with the words, "May the Lord Almighty grant us a quiet night and a good death."

When I first heard the monks pray these words, I found them a bit alarming and even distressing. Over time, I began to see them as words of grace and peace.

Today, God's Spirit lives in me. I can and will, by grace, remember this fact. *Spirit, enable me to know and rely on your life that is in me today, filling me to overflowing. May the work I do, the conversations I have, and whatever other tasks I engage in be touched by this reality.*

- *Do you ever think about your eventual death? If you do, how does it make you feel?*

- *How might the presence of the Spirit of resurrection bless you in such seasons of thought and prayer?*

53. BORN OF THE SPIRIT

The wind blows wherever it pleases. You hear its sound, but you cannot tell where it comes from or where it is going. So it is with everyone born of the Spirit. — John 3:8

The wind blows wherever it wishes, and we see the effect of that wind. Dust blows around, tree branches sway, clouds make their way across the sky. But we don't actually see moving air.

Jesus says that those who are born of the Spirit experience the Spirit in the same way that trees experience the wind. When we are rooted in the Spirit and fruitful due to his work in us, our lives are usually characterized by an element of the unexpected, the unpredictable, the surprising. A touch of mystery attends our journey. I have to admit, though, that sometimes I would rather reduce mystery and increase predictability. But for one born of the Spirit, this expectation for predictability isn't a holy impulse. When I'm seeking control, I'm usually not seeking God's reign or his way for my life. My inclination to control reduces my receptivity to the largeness of God's presence and God's work.

What does Jesus say about being born of the Spirit? "Jesus answered, 'Very truly I tell you, no one can enter the kingdom of God unless they are born of water and the Spirit. Flesh gives birth to flesh, but the Spirit gives birth to spirit. You should not be surprised at my saying, "You must be born again"'" (John 3:5–7).

Living in the kingdom of God requires more than our usual human perceptions and perspectives. We must be born from above just as surely as we have already been physically born here on earth. We must experience an inner awakening to God's kingdom reality that shapes our vision of life and work. We learn to be responsive to the moving of God's Spirit in us and through us. Like the wind.

- *As you move through your day, how might you allow your heart and mind to attend to the presence and voice of God with you?*

- *How might you trust in God's provision of guidance, inspiration, courage, and energy as you need it along the way?*

54. GOD-GIVEN LIFE

In the sight of God, who gives life to everything, and
of Christ Jesus, who while testifying before Pontius
Pilate made the good confession, I charge you.
— *1 Timothy 6:13*

God gives life to everything. Trees, plants, birds, and every
other living thing I see out my back window are all divinely
alive. Every living thing draws its life from the living God.
Life is the breath of God. Just as surely as the air that inflates
and exits my lungs keeps my body alive, so the breath of God's
Spirit keeps everything alive—keeps my soul alive. Paul said
to his audience in Athens, "In him we live and move and have
our being" (Acts 17:28). In God we have our very existence.

We live in a culture that offers a different message. It says we'll
only *really* be alive if we seek certain experiences or associate
with certain people or purchase certain products. It insists our
life is *elsewhere*. When the world warns us that we're not as
alive as we could be, it can sound convincing. But our life is
not in some other time or place or situation. Wherever we go,

there is air to breathe. Wherever we go, there is the living presence of God-with-us.

Excitement will come and go, but joy can arise from within us, where Christ has been making himself at home in each and every moment. In friendship with God through Christ, we are being renewed and revitalized day by day. Life is being renewed in us. What a beautiful, generous, reliable reality this is.

- *In what ways do you find yourself seeking vitality, excitement, or meaning in some other time, place, or situation?*

- *How might the presence of the living God with you now become the focus of everything you hunger and thirst for? How would you like to bring those desires into conversation with the living God?*

55. ALIVE IN THE SPIRIT

You, however, are not in the realm of the flesh but are in the realm of the Spirit, if indeed the Spirit of God lives in you. And if anyone does not have the Spirit of Christ, they do not belong to Christ. But if Christ is in you, then even though your body is subject to death because of sin, the Spirit gives life because of righteousness. And if the Spirit of him who raised Jesus from the dead is living in you, he who raised Christ from the dead will also give life to your mortal bodies because of his Spirit who lives in you.
— *Romans 8:9–11*

We are not living our lives—making ourselves at home—in the realm of the flesh but in the realm of the Spirit. If the Spirit of God lives in us (and the Spirit does), then our life is rooted in the life of God and is not separate from it. The Spirit who raised Jesus from the dead is alive in us. The Spirit will raise us where we have been lifeless.

When Paul says "if indeed the Spirit of God lives in you," the word *if* could also be translated as "since." I've sought to live my life in Christ for more than forty years now. I have the Spirit of Christ and I am alive in Christ. This isn't a question but rather a statement of faith and trust. I am given life—a phrase Paul uses twice in these verses—by the Spirit of Christ who lives in me.

What a remarkable reality! The Spirit who raised Jesus Christ from the dead is *in* me, bringing life to me today. Now. Here. Actually. The very Spirit of Christ gives life to this mortal body of mine because of and by his presence within me.

- *How alive do you feel these days?*

- *If you answered "very alive," take time to give thanks to the Spirit of Jesus who gives you life.*

- *If you answered "not very alive," how might you allow yourself to trust the real presence of the Spirit of Christ in you, bringing life to you? Take a few moments to talk with God about this.*

56. LIVING IN THE LIGHT OF GLORY

His disciples did not understand these things at first;
but when Jesus was glorified, then they remembered
that these things had been written of him and had
been done to him. — John 12:16 NRSV

The phrase "these things" refers to the events surrounding Jesus' entry into Jerusalem a week before he would be arrested, beaten, and crucified. The people's shouts of "Hosanna!" would soon be replaced with shouts of "Crucify him!" While the crowds were treating Jesus like a king coming into his kingdom, the disciples could never have envisioned how the week would end. And in those moments, they could not have understood the meaning of everything that was happening. Later, after Jesus was raised from dead in the power of God's Spirit, they would have a fresh perspective on all these things.

There are realities right in front of my eyes that I may not yet understand, but there will come a moment of encounter with Jesus and the reality of his glory that may shed light backward onto these things for me. I'm tempted to let my narrow perspective in a challenging moment become my whole vision of the present and the future. I need help to trust in the goodness of God and to hope for what I cannot yet see.

Just before he says that the disciples struggled to understand, the apostle John quotes the prophet Zechariah: "Do not be afraid, daughter of Zion. Look, your king is coming, sitting on a donkey's colt!" (John 12:15 NRSV). Jesus comes into Jerusalem humbly, riding on a young donkey rather than on a warhorse. Jesus may come into my situation humbly and gently rather than with overwhelming power. I may not feel immediately secure in moments like these, but there is power in his humble arrival. Jesus does not need to yell to be heard. He does not need to overwhelm to have influence.

- *As you look at your present season of life and faith in God, what is it that you do not quite understand?*

- *How do you respond when something doesn't make sense to you in the moment?*

- *How might the presence of Jesus, even coming gently and humbly, help you find hope, courage, and peace in this moment? Talk to him about this.*

57. THE POWER OF RECALLING GRACE

Praise the LORD, O my soul, and all that is within me, praise his holy Name. Praise the LORD, O my soul, and forget not all his benefits. Who forgives all your sin and heals all your infirmities; Who saves your life from the pit and crowns you with mercy and loving-kindness; Who satisfies you with good things, renewing your youth like an eagle's.
— Psalm 103:1–5 BCP2019

Psalm 103 is a psalm of David. His heart is full of praise as he remembers how many good things he experiences in the presence of God. My heart is also full of praise when I am fully awake to the multifaceted grace of God in my life. My heart becomes full of complaint when I become forgetful and let disappointing circumstances fill my awareness and my meditations.

Remembering that I am forgiven inspires worship; thinking that I am accused or condemned doesn't. Remembering that I am shepherded well in the midst of my weakness and illness provokes praise; feeling abandoned to what hinders or hampers me doesn't. Remembering that I have a Savior brightens my perspective; thinking that I am stuck in a dark pit doesn't.

Remembering that God is always honoring me with mercy and everlasting love fills my heart with joy; imagining that God is mostly impatient and disappointed with me doesn't. Remembering that the Lord is my portion and provides an abundance of goodness for my deepest needs encourages a bright perspective; believing myself to be mostly stuck in scarcity doesn't.

I need to often remember all God's benefits to me. I get into trouble when I am forgetful. Forgetting is like coasting downhill—it requires no intention or effort. Remembering requires remaining awake in my soul toward God and God's goodness. I can choose to remember, and it's good when I do. I can practice remembering. I can tell my soul to bless the Lord and remember how gracious, forgiving, caring, healing, protecting, honoring, and generous he is in my life.

- *In what specific ways are you remembering the goodness of God in your life right now?*
- *In what ways might you be tempted instead to rehearse certain hardships, losses, or weaknesses?*
- *What happens in your heart and in your interaction with God in each of these postures?*

58. THE HOLY ENERGY OF "SEEK FIRST"

All creatures look to you to give them their food at the proper time. When you give it to them, they gather it up; when you open your hand, they are satisfied with good things. — Psalm 104:27–28

All creatures. When I read these words, I tend to think of critters like the finches that are nesting in the eaves above our front door, or the hummingbirds that buzz around our backyard early in the morning, or our little dog, Lex, who brings us so much joy. But I am one of God's creatures. I am one of the living beings made by God. God nourishes me and provides for me just when I need him to ("at the proper time"). Who decides on that timing? God does. God opens his hand to me, and I receive good things that satisfy my hunger and thirst. I am so grateful!

Whatever satisfaction I experience in my life, it is the fruit of receiving what God gives. It is the fruit of divine generosity. It is the outcome of God's gracious initiative and activity. The invitation of Psalm 104 is profoundly simple: *Look to God.* I direct my attention to the God who is always with me. I focus my gaze on the face of God, the hand of God, the presence of God-with-us. I keep looking until grace meets me "at the proper time."

Whatever I need for today will be something given, not taken. I'm invited to lift my open hands into the presence of God throughout this day and to be ready and receptive. I'm invited to patient waiting, attentive waiting, ready waiting, like a sprinter in the blocks. When grace comes, I will know the presence of God's generous peace.

- *In this present moment, how do you feel hungry or thirsty in your soul?*

- *When you are hungry, how do you usually respond? Where do you take your hunger?*

- *How might you direct that hunger toward the One who has made you? What would it look like to wait patiently for grace to meet you here?*

59. THE LORD REMEMBERS US

The LORD remembers us and will bless us: He will bless his people Israel, he will bless the house of Aaron, he will bless those who fear the LORD—small and great alike. May the LORD cause you to flourish, both you and your children. May you be blessed by the LORD, the Maker of heaven and earth.
— Psalm 115:12–15

Our God is a God who remembers us. He has us in mind. His heart is to bless those who are seen as great and those who are seen as nobodies. Such human distinctions mean little to God. God is at work to make each and every one of us flourish. We can learn how to welcome and embrace this work so that flourishing becomes our home.

God blesses us and causes us to flourish so that we can be a blessing in the lives of those around us and serve them in ways that enable them to also flourish. The best way we can do that is to point them to the Flourisher in Chief. God, the Master

Artist, makes a beautiful and creative world of abundance. God is not one to skimp when it comes to creative work. And we *are* his creative work.

Today may we see God's hand of blessing in our lives, our relationships, and our work. May we find our way to trusting in divine abundance as the atmosphere of God's kingdom. May we and our children know this grace and peace.

- *In what ways have you been tempted to feel that God has forgotten you?*

- *What evidence do you see that God is remembering you to bless you?*

- *Take time to reflect and to converse with God, and make whatever requests or offerings of praise that arise within you.*

60. EMPOWERED TO ABIDE

I am the vine; you are the branches. If you remain in me and I in you, you will bear much fruit; apart from me you can do nothing. — John 15:5

I've sometimes misread this verse as a statement of my responsibility to abide in Christ. Understandable. But the vine precedes the branch. The vine gives birth to the branch. I love how Andrew Murray describes this reality in *Abide in Christ:*

> *"Let me listen and believe, until my whole being cries out, 'Jesus is indeed to me the True Vine, bearing me, nourishing me, supplying me, using me, and filling me to the full to make me bring forth fruit abundantly.' Then shall I not fear to say, 'I am indeed a branch to Jesus, the True Vine, abiding in Him, resting on Him, waiting for Him, serving Him, and living only that through me, too, He may show forth the riches of His grace, and give His fruit to a perishing world.'"**

---

* Andrew Murray, Abide in Christ (Fort Washington, PA: Christian Literature Crusade, 1968), 30.

Murray first focuses on what the vine does before focusing on what the branch does. Likewise, my first focus is not on my abiding activity but on the work of God in caring and providing for me so well. My abiding doesn't cause something as much as it receives something.

As the vine, Jesus carries me, provides for me, gives me what I need, uses me for his purposes, and fills me with every truly good thing. Because he has first loved me, I am then able to be a branch that abides in the vine, rests in him, waits for him, serves him, and lives my whole life in communion with him. In this way I can bear good and abundant fruit that truly lasts.

- *Are you tempted to hear this command to abide as a burdensome responsibility or as a standard to which you often don't measure up?*

- *Reflect on Murray's idea that our focus should first be on what the vine does rather than what we as branches do. In what ways does this encourage or help you?*

APPENDIX 1: ADVENT READING GUIDE

Made in the USA
Las Vegas, NV
14 December 2020

13166447R00085